TAPAS REVOLUTION

TAPAS REVOLUTION
OMAR ALLIBHOY

EBURY
PRESS

A lo mas valioso de esta vida: mi familia y amigos

10 9 8 7 6 5 4 3 2 1

Published in 2013 by Ebury Press, an imprint of Ebury Publishing
A Random House Group Company

The Random House Group Limited Reg. No. 954009

Addresses for companies within the Random House Group can be found at
www.randomhouse.co.uk

A CIP catalogue record for this book is available from the British Library

The Random House Group Limited supports the Forest Stewardship
Council® (FSC®), the leading international forest-certification
organisation. Our books carrying the FSC label are printed on
FSC®-certified paper. FSC is the only forest-certification scheme
supported by the leading environmental organisations, including
Greenpeace. Our paper procurement policy can be found at
www.randomhouse.co.uk/environment

Note on pimentón: Spanish pimentón or paprika is widely available and
comes in two varieties, sweet and hot.

To buy books by your favourite authors and register for offers visit
www.randomhouse.co.uk

Printed and bound in Italy by Printer Trento S.r.l

Design and art direction: Smith & Gilmour
Photography: Martin Poole
Food styling: Nicole Herft, Rachel Wood and Lucy O'Reilly
Props styling: Lydia Brun

ISBN 978-0-09-195125-2

CONTENTS

INTRODUCTION 6

1 APERITIVO 9

2 FISH 33

3 EGGS AND POULTRY 65

4 MEAT 87

5 VEGETABLES 117

6 SOUPS AND STEWS 145

7 RICE AND PULSES 163

8 DESSERTS AND SWEET THINGS 183

9 THE CHEF'S CUT 207

INDEX 221

INTRODUCTION

Para abrir boca...

What better pleasure is there in this world than to cook for others and then eat with them? Food, like life, is best shared with friends and loved ones, and tapas are the embodiment of that.

In this book you will find many of the recipes that I have cooked time and time again throughout my life. Long before I became a professional chef I was a keen home cook; today I pretty much cook every day, if not in my restaurant then definitely when I come home and need dinner. At heart I am a home cook rather than a chef, albeit one with an obsession with food. I have absorbed everything I could from everyone I've known and worked with along the way: my mum, my family, other chefs, restaurants in which I've eaten.

So, how do you define tapas? There are many theories as to its origins but originally a bar would serve a small, free tapa – usually a slice of cured meat or a piece of cheese – on a small plate with every drink. According to some sources these were used to cover wine glasses to keep flies out (the word 'tapa' originates from the word for 'to cover'). From these humble beginnings tapas have developed into a cuisine, and nowadays they can be small portions of pretty much any of the dishes that make up Spain's wonderful culinary legacy. A tapa can be hot or cold: a handful of marinated olives, a plate of crisp, deep-fried squid or a small dish of a gently simmering chorizo stew, mopped up with hunks of bread. A tapa is whatever you want it to be.

The beauty of tapas is that you can share them so easily with friends. Eating from the same plate enhances conversations, encourages adventurous eating and brings us all closer. Tapas developed to complement a convivial way of socialising: moving from bar to bar and enjoying a small plate of food with your drink means the proportion of food to alcohol is friendly!

Tapas Revolution, the name of my restaurant chain, was the result of the culture and food I grew up with. My parents loved travelling and took me to every corner of the world with them when I was a child. So I was curious about other cultures and other ways of eating. At the age of 21, I came to London and was fascinated by the way people socialised

in the UK, what they cooked and ate, at home and in restaurants. But mainly I was frustrated by the lack of good Spanish restaurants and couldn't understand why people didn't seem to cook any Spanish food at home. I decided that my mission was to put tapas on the map in the UK, and Tapas Revolution was born, with the stated aim of bringing the casual, convivial experience of the tapas bar to London.

I would argue that there is no such thing as 'authentic' Spanish cooking. Spanish food is constantly evolving and every region, restaurant, chef and home cook has its own different interpretation of the same dish. I have cooked these recipes hundreds, if not thousands, of times in search of the perfect result. For me taste and ease is sometimes more important than 'authenticity'. I want to show you that Spanish food is not complex or difficult and can be cooked every night. You won't have to travel the country looking for obscure and expensive ingredients, and I'm a firm believer in shortcuts – if you want to use a stock cube instead of fresh stock, go ahead! Sometimes you'll want to splash out and other times you'll be able to rustle up something fantastic using storecupboard ingredients – in fact some of Spain's finest ingredients can be found preserved in oil or brine in tins and jars. I'm naturally biased, of course (well, Spanish ingredients are the best in the world!), and I recommend stocking your cupboard with a few 'essentials' – Spanish olive oil, pimentón (smoked paprika), sherry, olives, rice. But the most important thing is that you get a feel for what you like and what you can achieve.

As we know, a tapa can be pretty much any Spanish dish, so the recipes in this book have been grouped together by ingredient. Forget about the idea of courses that follow on from each other – just put together any combination of dishes that you like. This is particularly good when it comes to cooking for a group of friends – vegetarian? No problem. Don't like seafood? Have a bit more chorizo. Desserts are often overlooked but Spain has a wonderful tradition of making sweet, milky puddings and tarts, so I wanted to offer several here. The final chapter is one that I just had to include: The Chef's Cut has slightly more unusual ingredients and more complex techniques. This is for the true revolutionaries among you.

APERITIVO ★ 1

ALMENDRAS
ALMONDS

Almonds are the most popular dried nut in Spain. In fact, Spain is the second largest producer of almonds in the world and our almonds are unparalleled. There are a number of Spanish varieties – all of excellent quality – but the best almond has to be Marcona.

ALMENDRAS SALADAS
SALTED ALMONDS

SERVES 4

PREPARATION TIME: 1 MINUTE

COOKING TIME: 5 MINUTES

50 ML WATER

1 TEASPOON ROCK SALT

200 G ALMONDS
[WITH OR WITHOUT SKIN]

1 Put the water and salt in a glass and give it a good stir.

2 Put the almonds in a wide pan over a high heat and dry-roast them, stirring all the time, for about 5 minutes or until the almonds are dark golden on both sides. At this point pour the salted water into the pan and give it a good stir. Because the pan is so hot the water should disappear within seconds creating a delicate, thin, salted crust around each almond. Remove from the heat and allow to cool down. These will keep in a glass jar for several months.

ALMENDRAS GARRAPIÑADAS
CARAMELIZED ALMONDS

SERVES 3–4

PREPARATION TIME: 1 MINUTE

COOKING TIME: 15 MINUTES

1 CUP ALMONDS
[WITH OR WITHOUT SKIN]

1 CUP CASTER SUGAR

1 CUP WATER

1 Put the almonds, sugar and water in a wide, heavy-based pan over a high heat. Bring to the boil and cook, stirring constantly, for about 15 minutes. Watch what is happening in the pan – first the sugar will melt into a light syrup, which will start to thicken as the water evaporates. Then it will start to crystallize (it will start to look like salt). Keep folding with the spoon so that the almonds are covered in sugar crystals, which will slowly turn to caramel.

2 When it has reached this stage, remove from the heat and tip out on to a sheet of baking parchment or a clean work surface. Spread out with a spoon so they don't stick to each other and allow to cool.

ACEITUNAS ALIÑADAS

MARINATED OLIVES

In Spain we are pretty much born eating olives. Spain is the biggest olive producer in the world so they are everywhere; you can't avoid them even if you wanted to. I'm always coming up with different ways to marinate them; the possibilities for transforming simple olives into a tasty snack are endless. Here are a few combinations that will not disappoint.

GREEN OLIVES WITH LEMON, OREGANO AND CHILLIES

SERVES 3–4 AS A TAPA

PREPARATION TIME: 5 MINUTES

JAR OF SPANISH GREEN OLIVES IN BRINE, ABOUT 300 G

100 ML MILD SPANISH OLIVE OIL

6 SPRIGS OF FRESH OREGANO

6 DRIED CAYENNE CHILLIES, FINELY CHOPPED

ZEST AND JUICE OF 1 LEMON

1 Drain the Spanish olives from the brine and place them in a bowl.

2 Whisk together all the remaining ingredients and mix with the olives. Serve immediately, but you can also keep them in an airtight container (ideally a glass jar with a lid) in the fridge for up to a month.

GREEN OLIVES WITH MANCHEGO, ROSEMARY AND GARLIC

SERVES 3–4 AS A TAPA

PREPARATION TIME: 5 MINUTES

JAR OF SPANISH GREEN OLIVES IN BRINE, ABOUT 300 G

50 G MANCHEGO CHEESE, DICED

4 GARLIC CLOVES, WHOLE AND UNPEELED

5 BLACK PEPPERCORNS

100 ML MILD SPANISH OLIVE OIL

2 FRESH BAY LEAVES

3 SPRIGS OF ROSEMARY

1 Drain the olives from the brine and place them in a bowl, along with the diced Manchego cheese.

2 Crush the garlic cloves and peppercorns with the flat blade of a knife and add them to the olives, along with the olive oil. Rub the herbs between your hands to release the essential oils before adding them to the bowl. Give everything a good stir so the oil becomes infused with all the flavours. Enjoy immediately – although they will keep in the fridge for at least 2 weeks. You can reuse the oil as a marinade for chicken or fish, or to drizzle over a salad.

NOTE
For a different flavour, roast the garlic cloves before adding to the olives.

Clockwise from bottom: Green olives with lemon, oregano and chillies; Black olives with red onion, paprika and cumin seeds; Green olives with manchego, rosemary and garlic

BLACK OLIVES WITH RED ONION, PAPRIKA AND CUMIN SEEDS

SERVES 3–4 AS A TAPA

PREPARATION TIME: 5 MINUTES

JAR OF SPANISH BLACK OLIVES IN BRINE, ABOUT 300 G

1/3 RED ONION, THINLY SLICED

1 TABLESPOON CUMIN SEEDS

1 TABLESPOON SWEET PAPRIKA

100 ML MILD SPANISH OLIVE OIL

1 Drain the olives from the brine and place them in a bowl, along with the sliced onion.

2 Use the flat blade of a knife to crush the cumin seeds and then add them to the jar with the paprika and olive oil; stir together. You can either nibble on these straight away or keep them in an airtight container (ideally a glass jar with a lid) in the fridge for up to 2 weeks. (Pictured on page 13.)

BOQUERONES
MARINATED ANCHOVIES

You will find these plump marinated anchovies in tapas bars throughout Spain, often served on a cocktail stick as a 'pincho'.

SERVES 4

PREPARATION TIME: 5 MINUTES

20 ANCHOVY FILLETS, PRESERVED IN VINEGAR

2 GARLIC CLOVES, FINELY CHOPPED

2 TABLESPOONS FRESHLY CHOPPED FLAT-LEAF PARSLEY

5 TABLESPOONS GOOD-QUALITY OLIVE OIL, PREFERABLY SPANISH

1 Drain the anchovies from their vinegar in a colander while you prepare the dressing.

2 Place the chopped garlic, parsley and olive oil in a small bowl and mix well. Lay the anchovies in a shallow dish and pour over the dressing so they are evenly covered.

3 Serve cold. You can either pop these straight into your mouth in one go or make a 'pincho' by spiking on a cocktail stick with a green olive or 'guindilla' chilli. These will keep in the fridge for up to a week.

PIMIENTOS DE PADRÓN

FRIED PADRÓN PEPPERS

SERVES 4–5 AS A TAPA
PREPARATION TIME: 1 MINUTE
COOKING TIME: 1 MINUTE

50 ML EXTRA-VIRGIN OLIVE OIL

200 G FRESH PADRÓN PEPPERS

SEA SALT FLAKES

These small green peppers are from Padrón in Galicia, northwest Spain, and they are somewhat of a speciality – grab them while they are in season, from July to September. We have a saying in Spain, 'pimientos de Padrón, unos pican y otros no'. It means 'Padrón peppers, some are hot and some are not', so prepare to play the game of Russian roulette; it's very difficult to tell which ones will blow your mouth off until you have crunched into them.

1 Put the olive oil in a wide frying pan over a high heat and heat until it is just at smoking point. Add the peppers (carefully, as the oil will be very hot) and stir with a long-handled spoon in case any of them spit and burn your hand. In hot oil, they should be cooked in 1 minute. The idea is to blister the skin of the peppers fairly quickly so they still have a fresh pepper flavour on the inside, with a lovely crisp, fried exterior.

2 Remove from the pan, drain on kitchen paper and sprinkle with salt flakes. Enjoy immediately, and good luck!

PAN CON AJO Y TOMATE

BREAD SCRUBBED WITH GARLIC AND TOMATO

SERVES 2

PREPARATION TIME: 2 MINUTES

COOKING TIME: 2 MINUTES

4 SLICES GOOD RUSTIC BREAD, SUCH AS SOURDOUGH OR CIABATTA

1 FAT GARLIC CLOVE

8 CHERRY TOMATOES

SEA SALT FLAKES

EXTRA VIRGIN OLIVE OIL, FOR DRIZZLING

OMAR'S NOTE

When you put this in your mouth, the first thing you taste is the pungent garlic on your tongue, followed by a hit of sea salt, then the tartness of the tomato and finally the sweetness of the olive oil. It's an all-round experience. Don't settle for fake *pan con ajo y tomate* – this is the real deal.

We eat this for breakfast, as an accompaniment to cured meats or to nibble on at the table. We even prepare our sandwiches like this, the way other people use butter. Remember, garlic wants to love you, so don't forget to love him back.

1 Toast the bread on both sides – use a griddle pan, a grill or just a plain old toaster. If you are doing a barbecue, chuck the bread slices on the grill for a lovely smoky flavour.

2 Leaving the skin on, slice off the flat end of the garlic clove. Cut the cherry tomatoes in half.

3 When the bread is toasted, scrub one side of the bread with the cut garlic and the other side with the cut side of the cherry tomatoes. Squeeze all the seeds and juice from the tomatoes by grating the tomato against the bread; discard the skin. I like to use just a little tomato but you can use more – it's up to you.

4 Place the toast tomato-side up (garlic-side down) on a plate, sprinkle with sea salt flakes and add a generous drizzle of olive oil.

SUGGESTION

In the Valencia region they make this without the tomato – just garlic, salt and olive oil. Try it – it's delicious with most things.

SALMOREJO
CHILLED TOMATO DIP

SERVES 4

PREPARATION TIME: 5 MINUTES

COOKING TIME: 5 MINUTES

1 EGG

50 G WHITE BREAD
(ABOUT 2 SLICES)

300 G RIPE TOMATOES,
ROUGHLY CHOPPED

1 GARLIC CLOVE

6 TABLESPOONS EXTRA
VIRGIN OLIVE OIL

1 TABLESPOON SHERRY VINEGAR

3 ICE CUBES

SALT AND FRESHLY GROUND
BLACK PEPPER

BREAD AND JAMÓN IBERICO,
TO SERVE

Salmorejo is traditionally from Seville. It is not a soup as many believe, but a dip. You will not believe how a few simple ingredients can be transformed into something delicious.

1 Bring a small pan of water to the boil and boil the egg for 5 minutes. Rinse under cold water and, when cool enough to handle, peel carefully and chop.

2 Roughly tear up the sliced bread and then put in a food processor or blender with the chopped tomatoes, half the chopped egg, garlic, olive oil, sherry vinegar and seasoning. Add about three ice cubes – this is to keep the mixture nice and cool as blenders can heat up the contents very quickly. Believe me, it really changes the dish if you don't add the ice cubes so don't be tempted to leave them out! Blend until you have a thick dip with a smooth texture.

3 Place in a bowl and sprinkle the remaining chopped boiled egg on top. Serve with bread for dipping and slices of jamón iberico. Another great way to serve this is with cooked peeled prawns.

MEMBRILLO
QUINCE JELLY

3 KG QUINCES

600 G CASTER SUGAR

JUICE OF 1 LEMON

200 ML WATER

OMAR'S NOTE

Membrillo goes very well with cheese – in particular our famous Spanish Manchego cheese. I also like to eat membrillo with fresh cottage cheese and olive oil and often use it in cheesecakes too.

My family has a house in the mountains near Madrid and it is where we all congregate every Christmas. We are completely spoiled in that you only have to walk out of the house to come across wonderful natural ingredients: mushrooms, asparagus, game, fish, nuts, wild fruits and berries. As you may well imagine, I'm very used to cooking with all of these wild ingredients and Christmas is a great time for making preserves for the year ahead which are shared between all the family members. So, back to the point, here is my foolproof recipe for quince jelly.

1 Wash and core the quinces and then chop into 3-cm pieces. You should end up with about 2 kg of prepared fruit. Put in a large heavy-based pan with the sugar and place over a medium to high heat. Stir the fruit from time to time so that it doesn't catch on the bottom of the pan. Quinces are quite hard and unlike other fruits such as strawberries, peaches or oranges, don't soften or release any liquid as quickly.

2 After about 15 minutes you will see the quince start to caramelize – at this point reduce the heat to low. Continue to cook at this low heat, stirring occasionally, for 1½ hours. After half an hour the quince will start to soften; after another hour it will become more like a paste. It should be dark brown in colour and have reduced to a quarter of the original amount. Add the lemon juice and water and cook for a further 10 minutes.

3 Your jelly is now ready. Pour into clean, sterilized jars; if properly sealed you will be able to keep for at least a year. Alternatively, you can pour into a baking tray lined with greaseproof paper. Once it has cooled and set firm you can turn out and slice into squares.

SUGGESTION

You can also make a softer, more spreadable paste, instead of this firm jelly. Simply add 2 glasses of water to the paste along with the lemon juice and purée with a hand blender until smooth. Continue to cook for another 5–10 minutes and then pour into sterilized jars as before.

Pictured overleaf.

ALMOGROTE GOMERO

CHEESE AND TOMATO PASTE

SERVES 3–4

PREPARATION TIME: 10 MINUTES

100 G MANCHEGO OR
OTHER HARD CHEESE

1 TOMATO, ROUGHLY CHOPPED

1 GARLIC CLOVE, FINELY CHOPPED

1 DRIED CAYENNE CHILLI,
OR 1 TEASPOON CHILLI POWDER

PINCH OF SALT

50 ML OLIVE OIL

This Canary island speciality is really quite addictive (especially if, like me, you love cheese). Try it with crudités and roasted vegetables or simply spread on toasted bread.

1 Traditionally this would be made using a pestle and mortar but you can also use a hand blender.

2 Chop the cheese into small cubes and blend or grind with the tomato, garlic, chilli, salt and oil until you have a smooth paste. Keep in an airtight container in the fridge for up to 5 days.

MI LIMONADA
LEMONADE WITH A TWIST

SERVES 4
PREPARATION TIME: 5 MINUTES
COOKING TIME: 5 MINUTES

3 LEMONS

5 HEAPED TABLESPOONS SUGAR

½ CUP WATER PLUS 500 ML

This is my signature lemonade and in summer I make a batch of this pretty much every week. Like gazpacho, it's one of those things that I always have in my fridge in the summer months, and when friends pop over they will most often ask, 'I don't suppose you have some of that lemonade you make...' Don't be tempted to call this traditional lemonade – it's my own invention.

1 Wash and peel one of the lemons, removing all the white pith from the lemon peel and cutting into strips; set the peel aside. Squeeze the juice of all the lemons into a bowl, making sure there are no seeds; set aside.

2 Place the sugar and ½ cup of water in a small pan over a medium heat. Bring to the boil and then let it reduce and bubble away until it becomes a golden caramel – make sure it doesn't turn too dark. At this point add the remaining water, lemon peel strips and juice so it becomes a light caramel and lemon syrup. Bring back to the boil, allow to simmer for 2 minutes and then remove from the heat.

3 Leave to cool down before chilling in the fridge. When you are ready to serve you can either drink it as it is or blend with crushed ice to make it 'granizado' style. The beauty of this lemonade, apart from the taste, is that it will keep for a good couple of weeks in the fridge.

Pictured overleaf.

MI SANGRÍA ESPECIAL
SPECIAL SANGRIA

SERVES 6

PREPARATION TIME: 15 MINUTES

COOKING TIME: 5 MINUTES

1 ORANGE

1 LEMON

1 PEACH OR 3 PLUMS,
STONED AND ROUGHLY CHOPPED

1 PEAR OR APPLE,
CORED AND ROUGHLY CHOPPED

200 G CASTER SUGAR

1/4 CINNAMON STICK

200 ML WATER

200 ML BRANDY

200 ML TRIPLE SEC

1 PUNNET (200 G)
STRAWBERRIES, HALVED

ICE

1 X 750-ML BOTTLE
SPANISH RED WINE

500 ML SPARKLING LEMONADE

I'm sure many of you have come across sangria before but, trust me – you won't have tried my special recipe! The idea behind this recipe is to make the fruit release more flavour into the sangria without wasting any fruit. It takes a little longer to prepare but I think you'll agree the effort is worth it. You can make a batch of the syrup and preserve the fruit in advance – it should keep for 3 weeks in the fridge.

1 First wash the orange and lemon and then peel off strips of the zest and cut into thin strips. Use a sharp knife to peel away the rest of the skin and pith and discard. Cut both fruits into segments. Place the orange and lemon segments and zest strips in a pan.

2 Add the remaining fruit (except the strawberries) to the pan along with the sugar, cinnamon stick, water, brandy and Triple Sec and bring to the boil. Allow to simmer for 1 minute, then remove from the heat and add the strawberries. Leave to cool and then chill in the fridge. All the essential oils and aromas of the fruit will infuse the syrup – this is the secret of this sangria.

3 Fill a large jug one-third with ice cubes and pour in enough of the fruit and syrup mix to come halfway up the jug. Add wine until the jug is nearly full and then add the lemonade to finish off. Stir with a long-handled spoon. Now sit back and enjoy!

FISH ★2

PESCAÍTO FRITO

FRIED FISH

SERVES 4

PREPARATION TIME: 10 MINUTES

COOKING TIME: 5 MINUTES

1 KG MIXED FISH, SUCH AS SQUID [FRESH OR FROZEN], WHITEBAIT, SPRATS, ANCHOVIES AND PRAWNS

150 G SEVILLIAN FLOUR [COARSEWHEAT FLOUR], SUPERFINE SEMOLINA OR CHICKPEA FLOUR [SEE NOTE]

MILD OLIVE OIL OR VEGETABLE OIL FOR FRYING

SALT

1 LEMON, QUARTERED [OPTIONAL]

ALIOLI, TO SERVE [SEE PAGE 44]

The Spanish *fritura* (a plate of fried food) is very delicate – crisp on the outside and moist on the inside. There is nothing better than fresh fried fish but it can be tricky to get right as there are so many variables: the freshness of the fish, the size of the pieces, the flour, the oil, the temperature, the cooking time, the draining... The reason why fried fish is so bloody good in southern Spain is purely because they have mastered this technique through sheer hard work and experience. And now I will tell you the secrets.

The perfect *fritura* should have a mix of fish – I like to use squid, prawns and then some other small fish such as anchovies or whitebait. I wouldn't recommend using anything bigger than 10 cm long.

1 If you are using frozen squid, always buy whole squid and let it thaw before cutting into rings yourself (chopped frozen squid tends to contain preservatives). If you are using fresh squid ask your fishmonger to clean it for you. Cut the body into rings and the tentacles into bite-sized pieces. Rinse the other fish in cold water and pat dry.

2 Spread the flour out in a shallow dish and start coating the squid rings, tentacles and fish. Make sure none of the pieces are stuck together and are completely covered with the flour – use more if necessary.

Continued overleaf.

3 Heat the oil in a large deep-sided pan until a cube of day-old bread dropped into it turns golden brown in 20–30 seconds. Alternatively heat a deep fryer to 190°C. One of the biggest issues when frying in a pan is that the temperature of the oil can drop quickly, which means you won't get that nice crispness on the outside. To avoid this, keep the oil as hot as you can and cook the fish in batches.

4 Put the floured fish pieces in the oil and fry for 1–1½ minutes, depending on the size. Stir carefully so that the pieces don't get stuck together and turn so that they brown on all sides. Remove from the oil with a slotted spoon and toss them in a bowl with some salt. You can drain on kitchen paper but this will make them soggier as any contact with a solid surface will make the steam escaping from inside of the fish condense and will be absorbed by the fried flour.

5 Serve immediately with alioli and lemon wedges (although I'm a purist and prefer my *fritura* without lemon).

NOTE

Coarse wheat flour, semolina flour or chickpea flour are all perfect for this recipe as they create an airy film around the fish, which allows the steam to escape, resulting in a crisper coating.

ALMEJAS AL AJO Y PEREJIL

CLAMS WITH GARLIC AND PARSLEY

SERVES 4–5 AS A TAPA

PREPARATION TIME: 10 MINUTES, PLUS SOAKING

COOKING TIME: 10 MINUTES

1 KG CLAMS

100 ML OLIVE OIL

6-8 GARLIC CLOVES, FINELY CHOPPED

3 DRIED CAYENNE CHILLIES, FINELY CHOPPED

10 SPRIGS OF FLAT-LEAF PARSLEY, FINELY CHOPPED

1 TEASPOON PLAIN FLOUR

150 ML WHITE WINE (I LIKE TO USE SOMETHING FRUITY – IT GOES WELL WITH THE FINISHED DISH TOO)

SALT AND FRESHLY GROUND BLACK PEPPER

OMAR'S NOTE

You may have picked up by now that the Spanish can sit and chat for hours while eating – we call this 'sobremesa'. Whether seated round a table or propped up at a tapas bar, it's a cultural and social thing for us. The great thing about clams is that they take longer to eat than to cook and are perfect for chatty, social occasions.

I love clams – well – I love shellfish in all its incarnations. A lot of Spanish cooking is about the quality and freshness of the ingredients and as the sea surrounds our peninsula, shellfish features heavily. We tend to do very little to it, except treat it with the respect it deserves. Garlic and parsley are classic shellfish flavourings and are all it takes to create a star dish.

1 Start by soaking the clams in cold water for about 20 minutes to allow them to release any sand trapped in their shells. Rinse thoroughly under cold water and discard any that are open, broken or that don't close firmly when tapped.

2 Put the oil in a large frying pan (wide enough to hold all the clams) and add the garlic and chillies. Place over a high heat and start frying from cold, until light golden. Add the chopped parsley, flour, salt and pepper and stir for 1 minute.

3 Pour in the white wine and stir vigorously so that the flour and wine are well combined. Add the cleaned clams, sauté a couple of times and cover with a lid for 2 minutes. Remove the lid and sauté a couple more times. By this time all the clams should have opened, if not, cover and cook for another minute. Discard any clams that refuse to open and serve immediately with lots of fresh bread to mop up the sauce.

ALMEJAS AL FINO CON JAMÓN

CLAMS WITH SHERRY AND SERRANO HAM

SERVES 4–5 AS A TAPA

PREPARATION TIME: 20 MINUTES, PLUS SOAKING

COOKING TIME: 10 MINUTES

1 KG CLAMS

100 ML OLIVE OIL

5 GARLIC CLOVES, FINELY CHOPPED

1 SHALLOT OR ½ SPANISH ONION, FINELY CHOPPED

6 SLICES JAMÓN SERRANO (CURED HAM), ROUGHLY CHOPPED

1 TEASPOON PLAIN FLOUR

1 TEASPOON HOT PIMENTÓN, ALTHOUGH THE SWEET VARIETY WILL DO AS WELL

150 ML FINO SHERRY (SEE NOTE)

2 TABLESPOONS FRESHLY CHOPPED FLAT-LEAF PARSLEY

SEA SALT AND FRESHLY GROUND BLACK PEPPER

Clams, garlic, pimentón, jamón and sherry… what could be more irresistible?

1 Start by soaking the clams in cold water for about 20 minutes to allow them to release any sand trapped in their shells. Rinse thoroughly under cold water and discard any that are open, broken or don't close when tapped firmly.

2 Heat the oil in a large frying pan (wide enough to hold all the clams) over a medium heat and add the garlic, onion and jamón. Cook until the onion is translucent, but not coloured.

3 Add the flour and pimentón and stir-fry for 20 seconds to cook the flour. Add the sherry, stirring all the time and then quickly flambé by setting light to the pan using a lighter or long matches. If you don't want to flambé the sherry don't worry, just cook for 1 minute so that the alcohol evaporates. Add the cleaned clams to the pan, turn up the heat and shake the pan vigorously, tossing the clams a couple of times. Season to taste and stir in the parsley, cover with a lid and cook for 2–3 minutes until the clams are fully opened (throw away any that remain closed). Stir again before serving with lots of fresh bread to soak up the sauce.

OMAR'S NOTE

Fino (which translates as refined) is the driest of all sherry varieties and should be drunk cold. This delicate sherry doesn't keep well after the bottle is opened, so make the best use of it.

GAMBAS AL AJILLO
PRAWNS WITH GARLIC

SERVES 2

PREPARATION TIME: 5 MINUTES

COOKING TIME: 5 MINUTES

12 LARGE RAW PRAWNS
IN THEIR SHELLS

3 GARLIC CLOVES, THINLY SLICED

100 ML OLIVE OIL

3 DRIED CAYENNE CHILLIES
(OR OTHER DRIED CHILLI)

SEA SALT FLAKES

1 TABLESPOON FRESHLY CHOPPED
FLAT-LEAF PARSLEY

You'll find this dish in pretty much every tapas bar in every coastal town in Spain, as well as in all the major cities. We love our fish and shellfish so much that the capital, Madrid (which is in the middle of mainland Spain), is a major fresh fish importer, second only to Tokyo. There are two ways of preparing this dish, depending on whether or not you want to peel the prawns before cooking. Traditionally this would be cooked in a flameproof terracotta dish, in which you then serve the prawns – if you don't have one you can use an ordinary frying pan and leave the heads and shells on. I love these either way.

1 Peel the prawns, leaving the tails intact (if you are using a frying pan you can cook the prawns in their shells). Sprinkle with a little sea salt.

2 Put the olive oil, garlic and chillies in the terracotta pot or frying pan and place over a high heat. When the garlic starts to turn golden, add the prawns. Cook for 1 minute on each side, until they just turn pink. Sprinkle over the chopped parsley and serve immediately in the terracotta pot. Take care not to burn yourself as the oil and the terracotta will stay hot for several minutes.

GAMBAS A LA PLANCHA

GRIDDLED PRAWNS

SERVES 2

PREPARATION TIME: 1 MINUTE

COOKING TIME: 4 MINUTES

1 HEAPED TABLESPOON ROCK SALT

8 LARGE RAW PRAWNS IN THEIR SHELLS

1 GARLIC CLOVE, FINELY CHOPPED

1 TEASPOON FRESHLY CHOPPED FLAT-LEAF PARSLEY

2 TABLESPOONS OLIVE OIL

1 LEMON WEDGE [OPTIONAL]

OMAR'S NOTE

Call me a purist but I prefer not to put anything on these – even lemon juice. The thing about lemon juice is that to me it has become a bit like dolloping ketchup, mayonnaise or chilli oil all over your food. I like to taste the pure flavour of what I've just cooked. Otherwise everything sort of starts to taste the same.

'A la plancha' is more of a technique than a recipe – you can cook anything this way, from pork chops, to langoustines, to asparagus.

1 Cooking a la plancha at home requires an extremely hot pan, as hot as it can get. Place a large heavy-based frying pan over a high heat. While the pan is heating up sprinkle the rock salt over the surface. When the pan is searing hot, place the prawns on top of the salt.

2 Mix the garlic, parsley and olive oil in a bowl.

3 After 2 minutes, drizzle the prawns with the garlic and parsley oil and turn them over. Because the pan is so hot the oil will immediately smoke a lot, but this will give the distinctive aroma of the plancha style of cooking. Cook the prawns for another minute or two, depending on the size.

4 If you like, squeeze over some lemon juice before transferring to a plate – although I have to say I prefer these just as they are.

NOTE

There are two techniques for cooking a la plancha: prawns cooked in their shells are cooked over a generous amount of rock salt so that the shellfish are hardly in full contact with the pan itself. When cooking a scallop, a razor clam or simply a lamb cutlet, the seasoning would be on the food and not on the pan, allowing the ingredient to caramelize properly.

ALIOLI
GARLIC MAYONNAISE

I'm not sure whether you would call this a sauce or a dip but this garlicky mayonnaise is a real favourite in Spain, particularly along the eastern Mediterranean coast, where it is traditionally from. As well as being delicious for dipping bread, alioli goes brilliantly well with many fish dishes, including Pescaito Frito (page 34) and Fideua (page 175). Its intense garlicky flavour is what makes it so addictive – as anyone knows, our love affair with garlic is profound. Over the years I have developed and perfected three different ways of making alioli, depending on how I want to use it.

Before we start, I'd like to point out that in my opinion the best alioli – and I've made a few in my time – is made with a Spanish olive oil produced from Arbequina olives. It is smooth and full of fresh fruit aromas as well as a little astringent.

MAYONNAISE-STYLE ALIOLI

SERVES 4 AS A TAPA ACCOMPANIMENT

PREPARATION TIME: 5 MINUTES

1 EGG (MAKE SURE YOU USE
ORGANIC OR FREE-RANGE),
SEPARATED

1 GARLIC CLOVE, PEELED AND
GERM DISCARDED (SEE OVERLEAF)

1/2 TEASPOON SALT

1 TEASPOON VINEGAR

200 ML OLIVE OIL (SEE OPPOSITE)

1 Put the egg yolk, garlic, salt and
vinegar in a jug and use a stick blender
to blitz for about 10 seconds. Keep
blending as you start adding the oil in
a thin stream. When you have added
half the oil it should start to thicken
up – at this point move the blender
up and down to make sure you get an
even alioli, until all the oil is used up.

2 Taste and adjust the seasoning and
serve. This alioli should last for up to
3 days in the fridge.

Left to right: My favourite alioli;
Mayonnaise-style alioli;
Traditional alioli

TRADITIONAL ALIOLI

SERVES 4 AS A TAPA ACCOMPANIMENT

PREPARATION TIME: 15 MINUTES

3 GARLIC CLOVES

1/2 TEASPOON SEA SALT
[FLAKE OR ROCK]

200 ML OLIVE OIL [SEE PAGE 44]

1 Peel your garlic cloves and halve them lengthways. Unless your garlic cloves are very young and fresh, it's a good idea to remove the garlic germ (the small shoots inside the clove) as they can make the garlic taste bitter, especially if it is not being cooked, as here. Discard the germs and chop the cloves finely.

2 Put the chopped garlic and salt in a mortar and pound it with a pestle until you have a very, very, very (I mean it!) smooth paste.

3 Now you need to add the oil. You can continue using the pestle and mortar if you wish or you can transfer the garlic paste to a larger bowl and use a whisk – the taste will be the same but using a whisk will result in a lighter-coloured alioli. Start adding the oil in a very thin stream, mixing all the time. The idea is to emulsify the olive oil with the salt and garlic paste. Keep adding the oil, a very little at a time to stop
it splitting, until the oil is used up.

4 Serve immediately, although you can make the alioli a day in advance and keep in the fridge.

MY FAVOURITE ALIOLI

SERVES 4 AS A TAPA ACCOMPANIMENT

PREPARATION TIME: 5 MINUTES

6 TABLESPOONS MILK

1 TEASPOON DIJON OR ENGLISH MUSTARD

1 GARLIC CLOVE

1/2 TEASPOON SALT

1 TEASPOON VINEGAR

200 ML OLIVE OIL
[SEE PAGE 44]

1 Put the milk, mustard, garlic, salt and vinegar in a jug and use a stick blender to blitz for about 10 seconds. Keep blending as you start adding the oil in a thin stream. When you have added half the oil it should start to thicken up – at this point move the blender up and down to make sure you get an even alioli, until all the oil is used up. Taste and adjust the seasoning and serve.

2 This alioli should last for up to 5 days in the fridge – about as long as milk keeps. The good thing about this version is that there is no risk of salmonella from eating raw egg. The texture and flavour of this alioli (which took me many years to achieve, truth be told) is the best I have tasted. Enjoy!

TRUCHAS A LA NAVARRA

TROUT WRAPPED IN SERRANO HAM

SERVES 2

PREPARATION TIME: 10 MINUTES

COOKING TIME: 10 MINUTES

2 TROUT, ABOUT 400 G EACH, CLEANED

4 LARGE SLICES JAMÓN SERRANO (CURED HAM)

100 ML OLIVE OIL

2 GARLIC CLOVES, THINLY SLICED

8 TINNED PIQUILLO PEPPERS

1 TABLESPOON FRESHLY CHOPPED FLAT-LEAF PARSLEY

50 ML SHERRY VINEGAR

SALT AND FRESHLY GROUND BLACK PEPPER

Trout is the most popular river fish, not just in Spain, but all over Europe. This recipe for trout wrapped in jamón serrano originally comes from Navarra and there are many variations.

1 Pat the trout dry with kitchen paper and then season the inside with salt and pepper. Wrap each trout with a couple of slices of jamón serrano and secure with a cocktail stick through the belly.

2 Place a non-stick pan over a medium to high heat and add half the olive oil. Pan-fry the trout for about 2 minutes on each side, depending on the size. Remove from the pan, discard the oil and wipe the pan clean with kitchen paper.

3 Return the pan to the heat and pour in the remaining olive oil. Fry the garlic until light golden, then add the piquillo peppers and cook for a couple of minutes. Remove the garlic and piquillos and set aside, leaving the oil in the pan. Add the chopped parsley to the pan and fry for about 20 seconds. Add the sherry vinegar and then pour the sauce over the trout. Top with the fried garlic and piquillo peppers and serve immediately.

NOTE
Trout, like a lot of river fish, has a very earthy taste which is why it works well with the jamón serrano and piquillo peppers.

FISH

TAPASREVOLUTION

CABALLA EN ESCABECHE

PICKLED MACKEREL

SERVES 4

PREPARATION TIME:
10 MINUTES, PLUS MARINATING

COOKING TIME: 10 MINUTES

4 SMALL MACKEREL

3 TABLESPOONS OLIVE OIL,
PLUS EXTRA FOR PAN-FRYING

1/2 SPANISH ONION,
THINLY SLICED

1 SMALL CARROT, CUT INTO
FINE STRIPS (JULIENNED)

4 GARLIC CLOVES

1 BAY LEAF

3 CRUSHED BLACK PEPPERCORNS

SPRIG OF FRESH THYME

1 TEASPOON SWEET PIMENTÓN

2 TABLESPOONS SHERRY
VINEGAR (ANY OTHER
WINE VINEGAR CAN BE USED
HERE IF YOU DON'T HAVE
SHERRY VINEGAR)

200 ML WHITE WINE

SEA SALT AND FRESHLY
GROUND BLACK PEPPER

OMAR'S NOTE

Eat this warm as soon as it is ready or cold the following day. You can also reheat in a microwave for 30 seconds (but do not reheat more than once).

Escabeche is a very popular technique in Spain that is used to preserve fish and game, from sardines to partridge and pheasant.

1 Ask your fishmonger to clean and fillet the mackerel for you. You can do this at home but, to be honest, it's a pain in the neck and the fishmonger will be able to do it much more quickly and efficiently!

2 Heat the olive oil in a pan over a medium heat and add the onion and carrot. Smash the garlic cloves, leaving the skin on, and add to the pan with the bay leaf. Cook for a couple of minutes and add the freshly crushed peppercorns, thyme and the sweet pimentón (you can use hot pimentón as well but I prefer the sweet variety for this recipe). After a few seconds stir in the sherry vinegar and wine – you need to add this quickly to stop the pimentón burning. Set aside.

3 Heat a drizzle of oil in a frying pan, season the fillets with salt and pepper and pan-fry over a high heat, skin-side down, for just for 1 minute – we don't want the fish to cook through at this stage. Remove the fillets from the pan and place skin-side down in a tight-fitting dish.

4 Bring the escabeche back to the boil and pour over the mackerel. Cover the dish with it with baking parchment or foil and leave to steam and marinate for a couple of hours before removing the baking parchment or foil.

BACALAO CON SAMFAINA

COD WITH PEPPERS, AUBERGINES AND TOMATOES

SERVES 4 AS A MAIN DISH

PREPARATION TIME: 5 MINUTES, PLUS SALTING

COOKING TIME: 1 HOUR

1 KG FRESH COD FILLET [SEE NOTE]

5-6 RED PEPPERS

1 AUBERGINE

200 ML OLIVE OIL

4 GARLIC CLOVES, THINLY SLICED

1 LARGE SPANISH ONION, THINLY SLICED

6 TOMATOES, GRATED OR PURÉED IN A BLENDER

1 TEASPOON SUGAR

SEA SALT AND FRESHLY GROUND BLACK PEPPER

In Spain we have been fishing and eating cod for centuries and it is probably the fish that I have cooked and eaten the most throughout my life. I love everything about it – the texture, the flavour, the fact that it has few bones and, when cooked properly, the skin has an incredible taste. It can handle strong, robust flavours too, such as this ratatouille-like sauce.

1 Cut the cod fillet into four portions and sprinkle with sea salt. Leave for a few hours to dehydrate slightly, then rinse away the salt and pat dry with kitchen paper. Preheat the oven to 200°C/ gas mark 6.

2 Rub the peppers and aubergine with a little olive oil, sprinkle with salt and place on a baking tray. Roast in the oven for 25 minutes, then place in a bowl and cover tightly with clingfilm.

3 Heat about one third of the olive oil in a large pan over a medium to high heat. Add the cod, skin-side down and pan-fry until the skin is golden, about 3 minutes. Remove from the pan and set aside.

4 Reduce the heat and add the remaining oil and sliced garlic. Cook for 1 minute and then add the onion and sweat for about 15 minutes.

5 Meanwhile, peel, seed and thinly slice the red peppers and peel and slice the aubergine; add to the pan. Increase the heat and add the grated tomatoes (don't bother to remove the skin and seeds – I never do and think the taste is pretty much the same). Add the sugar and salt and pepper and cook until the liquid has reduced down to about a quarter (this sauce has quite a strong, concentrated flavour).

6 Return the cod to the pan, skin-side up this time and reduce the heat. Cook for a further 5 minutes, until the cod is cooked through.

OMAR'S NOTE

In Spain 'bacalao' refers to both fresh cod and cured or salted cod, and for me (and most Spaniards) salted cod probably has the edge over fresh cod in terms of flavour. I've been eating cod since I was a child and I have noticed that the flavour has changed – it has less character than before. More and more people are eating cod and when it is farmed (as opposed to wild) it just doesn't taste as good. If you want to recapture some of that intensity of flavour, I recommend you try my trick of salting the cod to dehydrate it slightly. Always use good-quality sea salt (never table salt) and make sure you rinse and pat dry the fish afterwards. Go on – try it and you will feel and taste the difference.

You can also make this dish using salt cod. First rinse the cod well under cold water and then leave to soak in a large bowl of cold water in the fridge for at least 24 hours. You'll need to change the water at least three times in this time. Once the fish has been soaked, rinsed and patted dry, it is ready to use as above.

BACALAO A LA VIZCAÍNA

COD IN A RICH PEPPER SAUCE

SERVES 4 AS A MAIN DISH

PREPARATION TIME: 10 MINUTES

COOKING TIME: 30 MINUTES

1 KG COD FILLET

400 ML FISH STOCK OR WATER

1 BAY LEAF

100 ML OLIVE OIL

3 GARLIC CLOVES, THINLY SLICED

2 SMALL RED ONIONS, THINLY SLICED

2 RED PEPPERS, SEEDED AND CHOPPED OR 4 PIMIENTOS CHORICEROS [SEE NOTE]

50 G STALE WHITE BREAD, ROUGHLY CHOPPED

200 ML WHITE WINE

SALT AND FRESHLY GROUND BLACK PEPPER

OMAR'S NOTE

If you do get hold of the dried pimientos choriceros, you'll need to remove the seeds and stalk and then soak them in hot water. After 30 minutes, remove from the water, scrape the pulp from the inside (discarding the skin) and add to the pan when you add the bread. The result is delicious.

The Basques and cod go back a long way. They sailed the seas in search of it and salted it so they could eat it any time of the year. This recipe traditionally uses sun-dried red peppers (see Note), but you can use fresh peppers.

1 Cut the cod fillet into 8 pieces. Put them in a pan with the fish stock or water and bay leaf and place over a high heat. As soon as the liquid comes to the boil, remove the pan from the heat and set aside to cool. Lift the cod pieces out of the pan and set aside. Reserve the cooking liquid.

2 Heat the olive oil in a wide frying pan over a medium heat and add the garlic, onion and peppers. Cook for about 15 minutes, until they soften and turn golden in colour.

3 Add the stale bread and stir for a couple of minutes. Pour in the wine and cook until reduced by half, and follow with the reserved liquid from the cod. Bring to the boil and then simmer for 15 minutes before transferring to a blender. Blitz until you have a smooth sauce. You could also use an old-fashioned mouli to blend the sauce by hand.

4 Return the sauce to the pan along with the cod pieces and simmer over a low heat for 5 minutes. Season to taste and serve.

BACALAO AL AJOARRIERO
COD WITH PIQUILLO PEPPERS

SERVES 8 AS A TAPA

PREPARATION TIME: 5 MINUTES

COOKING TIME: 25 MINUTES

100 ML OLIVE OIL

6–8 GARLIC CLOVES, THINLY SLICED

1 SPANISH ONION, THINLY SLICED

1 TIN OR JAR OF PIQUILLO PEPPERS, APPROXIMATELY 15 PEPPERS OR 390 G

1 TEASPOON SWEET PIMENTÓN

1 TEASPOON SALT

1 TEASPOON SUGAR

4 TOMATOES, PURÉED IN A BLENDER

1 KG COD LOIN

OMAR'S NOTE

I love this recipe as much made with fresh green peppers instead of tinned piquillo peppers – the taste is different but really delicious.

This dish is from the Navarra region of Spain, where some of the best – if not THE best – vegetables in Spain are grown. Particularly famous are their piquillo peppers and white asparagus.

1 If you have time, cut the cod fillet into four portions and sprinkle with sea salt. Leave for a few hours to dehydrate slightly, then rinse away the salt and pat dry with kitchen paper. Cut into 2-cm pieces and set aside.

2 Heat the olive oil in a large pan over a medium heat and add the sliced garlic. Fry for a minute before adding the sliced onion and continue to cook for 5 minutes.

3 Drain the peppers of their juices and slice them thickly, making sure there are no seeds attached. Add to the pan and cook for a further 5 minutes and then add the pimentón, salt, sugar and puréed tomatoes. Simmer until the sauce has reduced by half.

4 Season the cod with a little salt and then add to the sauce in the pan. Cook for about 5 minutes, until the cod is just cooked, and then serve.

NOTE

In a Spanish pantry you will always find a wide variety of tins, from olives to tuna in oil, to piquillo peppers, white asparagus, cockles, mussels, sardines… You don't always have to cook with ingredients fresh from the market.

BACALAO AL PIL PIL

COD WITH GARLIC AND CHILLI SAUCE

SERVES 3 AS A MAIN DISH

PREPARATION TIME: 5 MINUTES

COOKING TIME: 30 MINUTES

600 G COD FILLET,
CUT INTO 3 PORTIONS

200 ML OLIVE OIL

4 GARLIC CLOVES,
SLICED (NOT TOO THIN)

2 DRIED CAYENNE CHILLIES

SALT

FRESH BREAD, TO SERVE

This is My Favourite Dish Ever. It is so good that I find it hard to explain why it is so special. Firstly, cod is my favourite fish. Secondly, the remaining ingredients, olive oil, garlic and chilli, when put together, are the three things that I love eating the most, especially when served with some really good bread. This dish has it all: a mellow texture, a delicate and fragrant sea aroma, a garlicky punch and a chilli kick – all brought together in perfect harmony by the olive oil.

1 Season the cod fillets with salt and set aside.

2 Traditionally for this recipe you would use a terracotta pot but it makes little difference, to be honest, so pour the olive oil into a pan that is just big enough to hold all the cod. Add the sliced garlic and dried cayenne chillies and start frying from cold. When the garlic turns golden, scoop out the cayenne chillies and garlic and set aside. Remove the pan from the heat to let the oil cool slightly, about 1 minute.

3 Add the cod fillets – they will fry at the beginning but will very quickly stop bubbling. The idea is to cook the loins in the infused oil at a very low temperature – like a confit. You will start to notice some liquid being released from the fish – this will form the base of our sauce and will be used to create an emulsion with the infused oil (like a mayonnaise). After 10 minutes

Continued overleaf.

reduce the heat to low, return the pan to the heat and let the cod cook, without letting it bubble, for 25 minutes.

4 To make the sauce, the easiest way is to remove the cod from the pan carefully and set aside. Use a large spoon to scoop out as much oil as possible from the pan; keep this oil to one side. Use a whisk or the bottom of a sieve (the tiny holes create good friction) to vigorously stir the juices in the bottom of the pan and gradually pour back in the oil that you removed, until the pil pil sauce is formed – it should start to look a bit like mayonnaise. You can also do this with the cod loins still in the pan – just scoop out the oil as before but shake the pan carefully but constantly (so as not to break up the fish) while pouring in the oil a little at a time.

5 Serve the cod loins with the sauce and top with the fried garlic and cayenne chillies. Dip the bread in the sauce – you will be amazed by the flavour.

BACALAO A LA SIDRA

COD IN CIDER

SERVES 4

PREPARATION TIME: 10 MINUTES

COOKING TIME: 30 MINUTES

100 ML OLIVE OIL

3 GARLIC CLOVES,
FINELY CHOPPED

1 ONION, FINELY CHOPPED

1 LEEK, TRIMMED AND
FINELY CHOPPED

1 CAYENNE CHILLI

1 TEASPOON SALT

1 TEASPOON CRUMBLED
FISH STOCK CUBE

1 HEAPED TEASPOON FLOUR

SMALL PINCH OF SAFFRON
STRANDS [OPTIONAL]

300 ML CLOUDY OR VINTAGE
CIDER [STILL AND DRY]

200 ML WATER

1 KG COD FILLET, CUT
INTO 4 PORTIONS

Apple trees are grown all over northern Spain and with apples comes cider. In Spain it is common to cook with all types of alcohol and cider is no exception. It makes fantastic sauces with a hint of acidity, but make sure you choose a non-fizzy, non-sugary type.

1 Preheat the oven to 180°C/gas mark 4. Heat the oil in a pan over a medium heat and gently fry the garlic, onion and leek for about 10 minutes, until translucent but not coloured.

2 Increase the heat to high and add the cayenne chilli, salt, fish stock, flour and saffron, if using, and cook, stirring, for 2 minutes.

3 Pour in the cider and cook until the liquid has reduced to one third; then add the water. Cook for a further 5 minutes before transferring the sauce to a blender. Blitz until the sauce is completely smooth.

4 Place the 4 cod pieces in a roasting tray, pour the sauce over the top and cook in the preheated oven for about 10 minutes or until cooked through.

BACALAO EN SALSA VERDE

COD WITH PEAS AND PARSLEY

SERVES 4 AS A MAIN DISH

PREPARATION TIME: 5 MINUTES

COOKING TIME: 20 MINUTES

100 ML OLIVE OIL

5 GARLIC CLOVES, THINLY SLICED

1 TEASPOON PLAIN FLOUR

50 ML WHITE WINE

200 ML FISH STOCK (FRESH OR FROM A STOCK CUBE)

SMALL BUNCH FLAT-LEAF PARSLEY, FINELY CHOPPED

1 X 142-G TIN COOKED PEAS, DRAINED OR 100 G FROZEN PEAS, DEFROSTED

1 KG COD FILLET, CUT INTO 4 PORTIONS

SEA SALT AND FRESHLY GROUND WHITE PEPPER

OMAR'S NOTE

If my fishmonger has them, I often buy a handful of clams to add to this dish – simply throw them into the pan just after adding the cod.

I hate to say this but my mum isn't the most gifted of cooks – she doesn't really enjoy cooking although she loves baking. However, there are about seven dishes that she cooks that cannot be beaten. This cod loin in parsley sauce is one of them. I've tried to better it but it can't be done, so here is her recipe.

1 Put the olive oil and garlic in a large frying pan and place over a medium heat (you want to start frying from cold so that the oil becomes infused with the garlic aroma). When the garlic starts to turn golden, add the flour and toast it for a minute or so before adding the white wine, stirring all the time. Add the fish stock, little by little, stirring constantly so you get a smooth sauce.

2 Add the chopped parsley and peas and bring to the boil. Season the cod fillets and then place in the pan, skin-side down, and reduce the heat to low.

3 Cook the fillets for 3 minutes, shaking the pan gently to release the juices from the fish – this will make the sauce even more delicate and flavoursome. Turn the fillets over and cook for a further 4 minutes.

DORADA A LA SAL

SEA BREAM BAKED IN SALT

SERVES 4

PREPARATION TIME: 5 MINUTES

COOKING TIME: 35–40 MINUTES

2 WHOLE SEA BREAM,
ABOUT 1.1 KG IN WEIGHT

2 KG ROCK SALT

1 LEMON

This way of cooking sea bream was created by the Moors in south-eastern Spain in the eighth century. It has since become one of the most famous fish dishes in any Spanish household or restaurant due to its simplicity and outstanding results. It's incredibly healthy as no fat is used whatsoever, and is really easy to make. Plus, I promise your kitchen won't smell fishy at all.

1 Ask your fishmonger to gut and clean the fish, opening up the fish as little as possible so that the salt doesn't get inside the cavity of the fish.

2 Mix the rock salt with a couple of tablespoons of water. This will help the salt stick together and create a good crust. Spread about one-third of the salt on a baking tray. Place the sea bream over the salt and completely cover with the remaining salt until all you can see of the fish is the tail.

3 Put the baking tray into the oven and set the temperature to 180°C/gas mark 4 (you do not need to preheat the oven). Bake for 35–40 minutes, keeping the oven door closed throughout the whole of the cooking time.

4 To serve, simply take the tray straight from the oven to the table, break the salt crust, peel away the fish skin and serve up the flesh. Squeeze over a little lemon juice and enjoy.

LUBINA A LA ESPALDA

SEA BASS WITH GARLIC AND VINEGAR

SERVES 1

PREPARATION TIME: 5 MINUTES

COOKING TIME: 6 MINUTES

1 WHOLE SEA BASS, ABOUT 500 G, GUTTED AND SCALED

3 TABLESPOONS OLIVE OIL

2 GARLIC CLOVES, FINELY CHOPPED

1 RED CHILLI (DRY OR FRESH), FINELY CHOPPED

PINCH OF SWEET PIMENTÓN

2 TABLESPOONS FRESHLY CHOPPED FLAT-LEAF PARSLEY

1 SPLASH VINEGAR

1 SPLASH WHITE WINE

SALT AND FRESHLY GROUND BLACK PEPPER

If I am ever home alone and feel like cooking fish, this is the recipe I will most likely go for. I just pop out to the fishmonger and get myself a portion-sized sea bass – all the other ingredients are store-cupboard basics. The key to this dish is the freshness of the fish itself, as there isn't much more to it than that. But it's also a masterclass on how to pan-fry a fillet of fish properly.

1 Ask your fishmonger to butterfly your sea bass for you. It will take him just a few seconds whereas you may end up spending much longer and, worse still, wasting a lot of fish. This way of opening the fish is called kiting, because you end up with a kite shape.

2 Place a large frying pan (wide enough to hold the butterflied sea bass) over a high heat and wait until it starts to smoke. Add a tablespoon of the olive oil and swirl it over the surface of the pan. Season the skin of the fish with salt and pepper and pick up the fish by the tail. Place the fish, skin-side down, into the smoking hot pan. Once all of the skin is in contact with the surface of the pan, apply some steady pressure on the top with your fingers so that the skin sticks to the pan – you don't want it to bend or curl up. Reduce the heat to medium.

3 From now on you don't have to touch the fish or the pan until the fish is cooked. Seriously, don't be tempted to turn it or move it around! The fish will talk to you through its colour; it has a pinkish colour when raw and turns opaque and white as it cooks – you'll see this happening. When the fish is nearly all white (this should take about 5–6 minutes), just lift it by the tail and, with the help of a spatula, transfer to a plate.

4 Heat the remaining olive oil in a separate pan over a medium to high heat and add the garlic and chilli. Fry for a couple of minutes until golden and then add the chopped parsley, pimentón, vinegar and wine (in that order). Let it all bubble for a few seconds and then pour it over the top of the fish.

EGGSANDPOULTRY ⭐³

HUEVOS ESTRELLADOS
CRASHED EGGS

SERVES 2

PREPARATION TIME: 5 MINUTES

COOKING TIME: 15 MINUTES

200 ML OLIVE OIL

1/2 SPANISH ONION, THINLY SLICED

2 MEDIUM POTATOES,
PEELED AND THINLY SLICED

2 GARLIC CLOVES, THINLY SLICED

4 EGGS

SALT AND FRESHLY GROUND
BLACK PEPPER

No visit to Madrid is complete without eating these crashed or broken eggs, as we call them. We eat them for lunch or dinner but you could also have them for breakfast or brunch. A crashed egg is somewhere between a fried and a scrambled egg – it 'crashes' because you crack open the egg some distance from the pan.

1 Heat the olive oil in a large non-stick frying pan over a medium to high heat and add the onion and potatoes. Fry for about 10 minutes, or until golden. Remove from the pan and set aside. Drain the oil from the pan, leaving just enough to fry the garlic. Add the garlic and fry for 30 seconds before returning the potatoes and onions to the pan.

2 Break the eggs one by one into the pan. You need to do this from a distance – at least 30 cm – so that the eggs crash into the mix. Season with salt and pepper and let them cook for a minute or so without stirring. They should still be very runny. Use a wooden spoon to carefully mix them in – remember you are not trying to make scrambled eggs! Serve immediately.

Continued overleaf.

SUGGESTIONS

Huevos estrellados is one of my favourite things to eat – onion, garlic potato and egg – pure comfort food. However, there are endless flavour combinations. Here are some of my favourites:

★ Morcilla de Burgos and chocolate – add one chopped morcilla sausage to the pan with the garlic and cook as above. Stir in 30 g grated dark chocolate just before adding the eggs.

★ Prawns and chorizo – add a handful of cooked peeled prawns and some chopped chorizo to the pan with the garlic.

★ Pimientos de Padrón and jamón serrano – add a handful Padrón peppers to the pan with the garlic and cook as above. Stir in some chopped jamón serrano (cured ham) just before adding the eggs.

HUEVOS FRITOS CON PUNTILLAS

FRIED EGGS

SERVES 1

PREPARATION TIME: 1 MINUTE

COOKING TIME: 1 MINUTE

200 ML EXTRA VIRGIN OLIVE OIL

2 EGGS

SEA SALT FLAKES

BREAD, TO SERVE

NOTE

'The simplest is not always the easiest'. This sentence is written on a board in all my restaurant kitchens – I can't think of a better recipe to illustrate this point than this one.

This simple fried egg dish is probably one of my top three dinners – I've eaten more of this than anything else. However, it's important to get the cooking technique right, as it's not as simple as it sounds. There are just three ingredients: oil, eggs and salt, so the success of the dish depends on the quality of the ingredients – use organic eggs, if possible. When you fry an egg at this high temperature the white becomes brown and crispy in parts – we call these crispy bits 'puntillas'.

1 Start by pouring the olive oil into a small frying pan (just slightly bigger than a fried egg). Ideally you want the oil to be the depth of two fingers. Place the pan over a high heat; the oil needs to reach a temperature of about 220°C. Take extra care and close the kitchen door if you want to avoid smoke in the rest of the house.

2 Break your egg into a glass first to check that there are no bits of shell. Quickly tip the egg into the super hot oil – do not drop it in from a height, as you will splash your hand with hot oil. You only need to cook the egg for 8 seconds so be ready with your slotted spoon. While it is cooking spoon a little oil over the top of the yolk. Remove from the pan quickly and move to a plate while you cook the second egg.

3 Sprinkle over some sea salt flakes and eat immediately with some good bread.

TORTILLA DE PATATAS

SPANISH OMELETTE

SERVES 6 AS A TAPA
PREPARATION TIME: 10 MINUTES
COOKING TIME: 25 MINUTES

2 LARGE OR 3–4 MEDIUM WAXY POTATOES (CHARLOTTE IS IDEAL), PEELED AND HALVED

1 SPANISH ONION, PEELED AND HALVED

8 EGGS

SALT

400 ML OLIVE OIL

As you may well guess, I have cooked thousands of tortillas in my life. There are about 25 different ways to cook tortilla and I have cooked them all: onion first, onion after, caramelized or not, no onion, potato slow-cooked or fried… the mind boggles. But after all my research, I believe this is the best recipe.

1 Thinly slice the potato halves, cut side down, so that you end up with half-circle shaped slices. Do the same with the onion.

2 Pour the olive oil into a deep frying pan and add the thinly sliced onion. Place over a high heat so you are cooking the onion from cold. Once the onion starts to sizzle (this should take about 5 minutes), add the sliced potatoes. Cook for about 15 minutes, stirring from time to time, until they are soft and cooked throughout. The potatoes and onions should have browned in some corners because of the contact with the bottom of the pan. If this hasn't happened drain away some of the oil and caramelize them a bit in the pan. Remove the potatoes and onions from the pan and set aside.

3 Break the eggs into a large bowl but don't whisk them; check there are no pieces of shell. Add the hot potatoes and onions to the eggs and season with salt while the potatoes are sitting on the top. Carefully mix through; use a fork to break up the eggs but don't over-mix – just

Continued on page 73.

VARIATION

For an 'instant' potato tortilla, let me introduce you to the best cheat I know: replace the fried potatoes in the recipe with a bag of good-quality plain crisps. Let them soak for a few minutes in the egg mixture and proceed as with the traditional tortilla. Don't be ashamed – we all need a shortcut sometimes, and the result is just so good!

give the mixture a few loops with a fork. If you can, leave the mixture to rest for half an hour to allow the flavours to develop.

4 To make the tortilla place a non-stick pan over a medium heat and add a drizzle of olive oil. When the pan is hot add the egg mixture. If you don't have a non-stick pan add the mixture to a very hot pan but reduce the heat to its lowest setting straight away; this will stop the tortilla sticking to the pan. Do not stir the contents of the pan!

5 Depending on the depth of your pan and the amount of heat from your stove, the cooking time will vary so you will need to use your judgement. After about 3 minutes you should be able to ease the tortilla from the edge of the pan using a fork or spatula. At this point, cover the pan with a plate (which should obviously be wider than the pan). Hold firmly with both hands and flip the pan over on to the plate. Slide the tortilla back into the pan for the other side to cook. Place back on the heat for another 2 minutes (I like it when the middle is still soft and a little runny).

NOTE
If this is the first time you have made a tortilla you might want to practise the flipping action with a plate and an empty pan first!

VARIATIONS
You can add all manner of flavourings to your tortilla if you like. Simply add to the egg mixture along with the potatoes and onions. Try small cubes of jamón serrano or chorizo, cooked petits pois or strips of tinned red pimientos.

REVUELTO DE AJETES

SCRAMBLED EGGS WITH YOUNG GARLIC

SERVES 4 AS A TAPA

PREPARATION TIME: 5 MINUTES

COOKING TIME: 8 MINUTES

1 BUNCH YOUNG GARLIC
[USE SPRING ONIONS IF YOUNG GARLIC IS OUT OF SEASON]

150 G OYSTER MUSHROOMS, WIPED CLEAN

1 TABLESPOON OLIVE OIL

3 GARLIC CLOVES, THINLY SLICED

2 TEASPOONS FRESHLY PICKED THYME LEAVES

4 EGGS

SEA SALT FLAKES AND FRESHLY GROUND BLACK PEPPER

BREAD, TO SERVE

OMAR'S NOTE

Scrambled eggs are really popular in Spain, particularly with wild asparagus or piquillo peppers and prawns. Just not for breakfast.

For most people in the UK, scrambled eggs are what you have for your Sunday breakfast, cooked with a little salt and pepper. In Spain we hardly ever eat eggs for breakfast, preferring to make them into something more special, such as these eggs with young garlic and oyster mushrooms. If you can't find young garlic, which is harvested before the cloves have matured, use spring onions instead.

1 Trim the young garlic or spring onions just a little and cut the stalks into three.

2 Heat the olive oil in a non-stick pan over a medium heat and add the young garlic or spring onions and oyster mushrooms; sauté for 3 minutes. Add the sliced garlic and thyme and fry for a couple more minutes.

3 Season with salt and pepper and then break the eggs into the pan (never whisk or season the eggs before adding to the pan). Scramble the eggs gently – don't over-mix as you still want to be able to make out the yolk from the white – this should take about 1–2 minutes if, like me, you like your eggs soft; cook for longer if you prefer. Enjoy with lots of good bread.

PIPERRADA CON HUEVOS

PAN-FRIED PEPPERS BAKED WITH EGGS

SERVES 4 AS A TAPA

PREPARATION TIME: 10 MINUTES

COOKING TIME: 35 MINUTES

100 ML OLIVE OIL

5 GARLIC CLOVES, THINLY SLICED

3 ONIONS, THINLY SLICED

2 RED PEPPERS, SEEDED AND THINLY SLICED

2 GREEN PEPPERS, SEEDED AND THINLY SLICED

1 TEASPOON SALT

1 TEASPOON SUGAR

4 SPRIGS OF FRESH THYME, LEAVES PICKED

3 TOMATOES, FINELY CHOPPED OR GRATED OR 1 X 400-G TIN CHOPPED TOMATOES

4 EGGS (OR 8 IF YOU ARE REALLY HUNGRY)

Throughout the area from the Basque country to Madrid people have a special relationship with peppers. They grow them extremely well, in all colours, varieties and shapes. This dish could only be from northern Spain.

1 Preheat the oven to 180°C/gas mark 4. Put the olive oil in a wide frying pan and place over a medium to high heat. Add the garlic and fry for 30 seconds before adding the sliced onions and peppers.

2 Cook, stirring, for about 10 minutes and then add the salt, sugar, picked thyme leaves and chopped tomatoes and cook for another 15 minutes over a medium heat.

3 Pour the piperrada mixture into an ovenproof dish or individual heatproof plates (this would traditionally be cooked in terracotta dishes). Crack the eggs on top, season and bake in the oven for 7 minutes or until the egg is cooked to your liking.

ALITAS DE POLLO AL VINO DULCE

CHICKEN WINGS WITH SWEET WINE

SERVES 6 AS A TAPA

PREPARATION TIME: 5 MINUTES

COOKING TIME: 20 MINUTES

500 G CHICKEN WINGS

5 TABLESPOONS OLIVE OIL

1/2 SPANISH ONION, THINLY SLICED

3 GARLIC CLOVES, THINLY SLICED

100 G DRIED PRUNES, STONED

2 SPRIGS OF FRESH THYME, LEAVES PICKED

100 ML SWEET SHERRY, SUCH AS PEDRO XIMÉNEZ OR MOSCATEL [SEE NOTE]

SEA SALT AND FRESHLY GROUND BLACK PEPPER

In Spain we love eating with our hands, whether it's tearing the head of a whole prawn and sucking out the juices or eating chicken wings with our fingers. These succulent chicken wings glazed in a syrupy sherry and prune sauce will have you eating like a true Spaniard. Leave your manners under the table and do battle!

1 Clean the chicken wings and separate them at the joint. Heat the olive oil in a wide frying pan over a medium to high heat and add the chicken wings. Cook until they are a dark golden colour, remove from the pan and set aside.

2 Reduce the heat and add the onion and garlic to the same pan. Cook for a few minutes until the onion turns golden brown. Return the chicken wings to the pan.

3 Season with salt and pepper and add the prunes (chop a few if you wish) and fresh thyme. Add the sherry to the pan and flambé by setting light to the pan using a lighter or long matches. (If you don't want to flambé the sherry, don't worry, just cook for a couple of minutes so that the alcohol evaporates). Add a small glass of water and cook for a few more minutes until the liquid has reduced down.

A NOTE ON SHERRY

I'm often amazed that sherry has such a bad reputation outside of Spain so let me try to put you straight. Sherry is special for many reasons and there is a whole world of different styles, depending on the grape, the climate and how it is aged. However, apart from the flavour, there is one characteristic of sherry that really plays on our side when it comes to cooking. The result is that, fino aside, sherry doesn't go off once the bottle is opened – the flavour actually develops, matures and tastes great for a long time. So, I would say you can afford to keep at least two varieties of sherry in your cupboard. I'm a firm believer in buying the best you can afford but at the same time you shouldn't need to break the bank to eat well. I've tried and tested pretty much every supermarket ingredient and when it comes to wine for cooking – and particularly sherry – don't use the cheapest one available. The difference in taste, particularly in a dish like this one, will be worth every penny.

POLLO AL AJILLO

GARLICKY CHICKEN

PREPARATION TIME: 10 MINUTES

COOKING TIME: 30–40 MINUTES

1 ORGANIC OR FREE-RANGE CHICKEN, ABOUT 1.5 KG, OR 1 KG CHICKEN THIGHS

100 ML OLIVE OIL

1 LARGE HEAD OF GARLIC, CLOVES CRUSHED

1 BAY LEAF

10 SPRIGS OF THYME, LEAVES PICKED

1 SPRIG OF ROSEMARY, LEAVES PICKED

200 ML MANZANILLA SHERRY

SALT AND FRESHLY GROUND BLACK PEPPER

As you probably know by now, in Spain we love our garlic. We love a good chicken too – perhaps this is why this is one of the most popular dishes on any tapas bar menu. It's also very popular done with rabbit – if rabbit is available, I recommend you give it a try. If you like a bit more sauce, add a chopped onion along with the garlic and a small glass of water and reduce until you have the right amount of sauce – perfect for dipping fresh bread into!

1 If using a whole chicken, joint it into 8 pieces and then cut any large joints in half to give you about 10–12 pieces. Leave the skin on. Season generously with salt and pepper.

2 Heat the olive oil in a large, heavy-based pan or casserole over a medium heat and add the chicken pieces. Fry the chicken on all sides until light golden; this should take about 15 minutes. Add the garlic and herbs and continue to cook until the chicken has taken on a dark brown colour, about 10 minutes.

3 Add the sherry and stir to deglaze the bottom of the pan. Cook for another 5 minutes, until the sauce has reduced right down to almost nothing. Taste and adjust the seasoning and serve.

POLLO AL CHILINDRON

CHICKEN AND RED PEPPER STEW

SERVES 4

PREPARATION TIME: 15 MINUTES

COOKING TIME: 1 HOUR

1 ORGANIC OR FREE-RANGE CHICKEN, ABOUT 1.2 KG

100 ML OLIVE OIL

7 GARLIC CLOVES, THINLY SLICED

1 LARGE OR 2 SMALL RED PEPPERS, SEEDED AND THINLY SLICED

1 LARGE SPANISH ONION, FINELY SLICED

100 G JAMÓN SERRANO PIECES (OPTIONAL)

2 BAY LEAVES

1 TEASPOON SUGAR

5 TOMATOES, GRATED

200 ML WHITE WINE

SALT AND FRESHLY GROUND BLACK PEPPER

This is a wonderful traditional chicken dish and is one of those dishes that you can probably make any time, as the ingredients are always readily available. Beware, the rich tomatoey sauce is quite addictive!

1 Joint the chicken into pieces, leaving it on the bone and with the skin on for a really good flavour. Season well with salt and pepper.

2 Heat the olive oil in a large, heavy-based pan over a high heat and add the chicken pieces. Fry on all sides until golden brown, remove from the pan and set aside.

3 Reduce the heat to medium and, in the same oil, fry the garlic, red pepper, onion and jamón serrano, if using. Cook for 5–10 minutes, until the onion is translucent. Add the bay leaves, sugar and grated tomatoes and cook for a further 10 minutes until you have a rich sauce.

4 Pour in the white wine and return the chicken to the pan. Leave to simmer over a low heat for 30 minutes, or until the chicken is tender. Taste and adjust the seasoning and serve.

POLLO EN PEPITORIA

MOORISH CHICKEN

SERVES 4
PREPARATION TIME: 10 MINUTES
COOKING TIME: 30–40 MINUTES

1 TABLESPOON WHOLE
ALMONDS, SKINNED

OLIVE OIL, FOR FRYING

2 SLICES OF BREAD

SPRIG OF FRESH PARSLEY

2 EGGS

8–10 ORGANIC OR FREE-RANGE
CHICKEN THIGHS OR PIECES,
SKIN ON

2 GARLIC CLOVES,
FINELY CHOPPED

1 SMALL SPANISH ONION,
FINELY CHOPPED

1 BAY LEAF

SPRIG OF THYME

1 TOMATO, CHOPPED

1 TEASPOON GROUND CUMIN

PINCH OF SAFFRON STRANDS

PINCH OF FRESHLY
GRATED NUTMEG

175 ML BRANDY

SALT AND FRESHLY GROUND
BLACK PEPPER

NOTE
You can blend the sauce
before adding the chicken
for a more refined touch.

Spanish gastronomy has been greatly influenced by the Moors and this dish is a great representation of their influences. Traditionally this would have been made using a broiler hen.

1 Start by toasting the almonds in a frying pan placed over a medium heat. After a few minutes they should turn golden – remove from the pan and set aside. Add a little olive oil to the pan and fry the slices of bread until golden. Drain on kitchen paper, then cut into rough pieces and set aside. Fry the parsley in a little more olive oil and set aside too.

2 Bring a pan of water to the boil and cook the eggs for 5 minutes. Drain and rinse under cold water until cool enough to peel. Quarter.

3 Add 4 tablespoons of olive oil to the frying pan and sear the chicken pieces on all sides until dark and golden; remove from the pan. Do this in batches if necessary. Again, drizzle a little more oil in the pan and add the garlic, onion, bay leaf and thyme. Cook for about 5 minutes, until the onion starts to caramelize and then stir in the tomato, cumin, saffron, nutmeg and seasoning.

4 Pour over the brandy and let the sauce reduce down a little before adding about 200 ml of water. Bring the sauce back to the boil and return the chicken pieces to the pan along with the almonds, fried bread pieces, eggs and fried parsley. Leave to simmer for about 15 minutes, or until the chicken is cooked.

POLLO CON SALSA DE ACEITUNAS ESPAÑOLAS

CHICKEN WITH SPANISH OLIVES

SERVES 4

PREPARATION TIME: 10 MINUTES

COOKING TIME: 30–40 MINUTES

8 FREE-RANGE CHICKEN THIGHS

50 ML SPANISH OLIVE OIL

6–8 GARLIC CLOVES, THINLY SLICED

1 SPANISH ONION, THINLY SLICED

1 TABLESPOON FLOUR

2 SPRIGS OF FRESH ROSEMARY

3 TABLESPOONS BRANDY

1 GLASS OF WHITE WINE

200 ML WATER OR CHICKEN STOCK, IF YOU HAVE IT

150 G PITTED GREEN AND PURPLE SPANISH OLIVES

SALT AND FRESHLY GROUND BLACK PEPPER

Braised chicken with Spanish olives – a classic.

1 Season the chicken thighs with salt and pepper. Place a large heavy-based pan over a high heat and add the olive oil. Brown the chicken thighs all over, placing them skin-side down first as they will release a bit of fat, which will turn the chicken a lovely golden brown. Remove from the pan and set aside.

2 Reduce the heat to medium. Add the garlic and onion and fry until it starts to colour. Now sprinkle over the flour and cook for 1 minute, stirring all the time. Add the rosemary sprigs and then quickly flambé by setting light to the pan with a lighter or some long matches. Add the wine and stir into the flour until there are no lumps. Return the chicken thighs to the pan and simmer for a couple of minutes until the wine has reduced by half and some of the alcohol has evaporated.

3 Stir in the water or stock, add the olives and some black pepper, cover and simmer for about 20 minutes, until the chicken is tender and you have a juicy and rich sauce. Taste for seasoning – *buen provecho*!

POLLO CON UVAS, VINO TINTO Y CASTAÑAS

CHICKEN WITH GRAPES, RED WINE AND CHESTNUTS

SERVES 3

PREPARATION TIME: 20 MINUTES

COOKING TIME: 50 MINUTES

9 FRESH CHESTNUTS

1 ORGANIC OR FREE-RANGE CHICKEN, ABOUT 1.5 KG, OR 1 KG CHICKEN THIGHS

100 ML OLIVE OIL

5 GARLIC CLOVES, FINELY CHOPPED

½ SPANISH ONION, FINELY CHOPPED

1 STICK OF CELERY, FINELY CHOPPED

8 SAGE LEAVES

25 ML BRANDY

200 ML RED WINE

200 ML WATER

30 GRAPES (RED OR GREEN, WHATEVER IS AVAILABLE)

SALT AND FRESHLY GROUND BLACK PEPPER

This particular chicken dish uses fresh chestnuts so it's one to save for when they are in season. As soon as I see chestnuts in the shops (from November to February) this dish pops straight into my head.

1 Bring a large pan of water to the boil. Cut the chestnuts in half with a sharp knife and throw them into the boiling water; cook for 10 minutes. Drain and leave to cool. Use a pair of pliers to squeeze the chestnut halves – the skin and shell should come clean away. If you are using a whole chicken, joint it into 8 pieces and then cut any large joints in half to give you about 10–12 pieces. Season generously with salt and pepper.

2 Heat the olive oil in a large, heavy-based pan over a medium to high heat and add the chicken pieces. Fry on all sides until golden, about 15 minutes. Add the garlic and peeled chestnuts; after 1 minute add the chopped onion and celery. Cook, stirring, for 10 minutes until the onion and celery have softened and turned golden.

3 Add the sage leaves, brandy and red wine and flambé the pan: use a lighter or long matches to set light to the alcohol as soon as you add it to the pan. Reduce until there is no liquid left and then add the water. Taste and add more seasoning and then add the grapes. Reduce the heat and leave to simmer for 20 minutes.

MEAT⭐4

CHORIZO A LA SIDRA

CHORIZO WITH CIDER

SERVES 8 AS A TAPA

PREPARATION TIME: 1 MINUTE

COOKING TIME: 30 MINUTES

4 FRESH SPICY
CHORIZO SAUSAGES

500 ML VINTAGE CIDER
(STILL AND DRY)

BREAD, TO SERVE

Chorizo sausage cooked in cider is one of the easiest tapas to make – there are only two ingredients and no chopping involved. All you need is a pan and a bottle opener. And don't forget the bread!

1 Place the chorizo sausages in a small pan (they should fit snugly) and pour over the cider. Cook over a high heat until the cider reduces down into a rich syrup – this should take about 30 minutes. Alternatively you can reduce the heat to low and leave the sausages cooking for up to an hour – they will be just as tasty and tender.

2 Cut the chorizo into thick slices and serve hot with good bread.

NOTE

Chorizo is well known outside of Spain but few realise how many different types there are, depending on the amount of spice (pimentón) used and whether it is smoked or unsmoked, fresh or cured... It's incredibly versatile as it can be flashed under a hot grill for 2 minutes, cooked in cider or wine for half an hour or stewed for several hours. To me, whichever way it is prepared, chorizo always tastes delicious. Make sure you use fresh chorizo for this recipe as dry-cured chorizo will become very hard.

CROQUETAS DE JAMÓN

HAM CROQUETTES

SERVES 6 / MAKES 24

PREPARATION TIME: 20 MINUTES,
PLUS CHILLING

COOKING TIME: 1 HOUR

50 G BUTTER

1/3 SMALL SPANISH ONION,
FINELY CHOPPED

70 G JAMÓN SERRANO
(CURED HAM)

800 ML FULL-FAT MILK

60 G PLAIN FLOUR,
PLUS EXTRA FOR ROLLING

PINCH OF FRESHLY
GRATED NUTMEG

1 TEASPOON SALT

PINCH OF GROUND WHITE
PEPPER (GROUND BLACK
PEPPER WILL ALSO DO)

2 EGGS

50 G DRIED BREADCRUMBS

VEGETABLE OIL FOR DEEP-FRYING

NOTE

Enjoy the unctuous
creaminess of real Spanish
ham croquetas. *Salud*!

These deep-fried béchamel balls were
sent from heaven to make us mortals a bit
happier. Croquetas are famous throughout
Spain – customers rave about the taste and
texture while those who make them know
that the best things in life come at a price –
yes, they are time-consuming to prepare.
I could tell you that this croquetas recipe
is a treasured family recipe but the truth
is that I have developed it over the years
myself, and after endless research and
cooking them literally hundreds of times,
I believe these are among the best you
will find. Enjoy!

1 Melt the butter in a pan over a medium heat
and add the chopped onion and jamón serrano.
Cook for a few minutes until the onion turns
translucent but not coloured. Meanwhile, in a
separate pan, bring the milk almost to boiling
point and then set aside.

2 Add the flour to the onion and cook for 5
minutes, stirring, until the flour has toasted
a bit. Add the hot milk little by little, whisking
all the time, to make a thick roux. Keep going
until you have added all the milk and you have
a smooth and silky béchamel. When it comes
back to the boil reduce the heat to low and add
the nutmeg, salt and pepper. Leave to simmer
for about 40 minutes, whisking to make sure
it doesn't stick to the bottom of the pan. Taste
and adjust the seasoning if necessary.

Continued on page 94.

Continued from page 90.

3 Line the bottom of a baking tray with baking parchment and then pour the béchamel into the baking tray. Spread it out and then immediately place a layer of cling film directly on top, making sure the cling flim is touching the surface of the béchamel as this will stop a skin from forming. Transfer to the fridge to chill completely.

4 After 3 hours the béchamel should be firm enough to handle. Peel off the cling film, turn the béchamel out on to a floured surface and carefully peel away the baking parchment. Sprinkle with a little more flour and use a knife to cut the béchamel into strips and then small squares, about 4 cm square. Dust your hands with flour and roll these little squares into balls between your hands.

5 Beat the egg in a bowl and spread the breadcrumbs out on a plate. Dip each ball in the egg and then roll in the breadcrumbs before placing on a clean plate. You can chill these in the fridge at this point, if you want to cook them later (or freeze them for next time).

6 Heat the oil in a large deep pan until it reaches 180°C. If you don't have a thermometer you can check whether the oil is ready by dropping a small square of bread into the oil – it should turn golden in about 30 seconds. Fry the croquetas in small batches until they are golden and crisp (this should take about 1 ½ minutes). Remove and drain on kitchen paper while you cook the rest.

CONEJO A LA CAZADORA

HUNTER'S RABBIT

SERVES 4

PREPARATION TIME: 15 MINUTES

COOKING TIME: 55 MINUTES

100 ML OLIVE OIL

1 RABBIT OR HARE,
JOINTED INTO 8–10 PIECES

1 LARGE SPANISH ONION,
ROUGHLY CHOPPED

1 HEAD GARLIC, SLICED IN
HALF THROUGH THE EQUATOR

4 CARROTS, PEELED AND
ROUGHLY CHOPPED

100 G LARDONS OR SMOKED
BACON PIECES

150 G OYSTER MUSHROOMS,
CLEANED

2 TABLESPOONS PLAIN FLOUR

5 SPRIGS OF THYME,
LEAVES PICKED

1 BAY LEAF

250 ML WHITE WINE

1 CHICKEN STOCK CUBE

1 TABLESPOON SUGAR

NOTE

Cooking times vary
depending on whether
the rabbit is farmed or
wild: wild will take a
little longer to cook.

Rabbit is often eaten in Spain and this
recipe for a traditional hunters-style stew
is hearty and full of flavour. You should be
able to get rabbit from any good butcher.
You could also try making this recipe with
one whole chicken, jointed into eight pieces,
or four quails.

1 Heat the olive oil in a large, heavy-based pan
over a medium heat and add the rabbit pieces.
Fry until the rabbit is nicely browned all over.
Remove from the pan and set aside.

2 Add the onion, garlic, carrot, bacon and
mushrooms to the pan and cook until the
vegetables are caramelized and dark golden
in colour.

3 Reduce the heat to medium and stir in the
flour, thyme and bay leaf. After 30 seconds
return the rabbit pieces to the pan and deglaze
the pan with the white wine, scraping any sticky
bits from the bottom. Boil for about 30 seconds
so that the alcohol evaporates and then stir in
2 glasses of water, the chicken stock cube
and sugar.

4 Cover the pan with a lid, reduce the heat and
leave to simmer for about 40 minutes, or until
the rabbit is tender and the sauce looks shiny
and is the consistency of double cream.

ALBÓNDIGAS EN SALSA

MEATBALLS

SERVES 4

PREPARATION TIME: 15 MINUTES

COOKING TIME: 1 HOUR

FOR THE MEATBALLS

3 SLICES WHITE BREAD

100 ML MILK

250 G MINCED BEEF

250 G MINCED PORK

¼ SPANISH ONION, FINELY CHOPPED

1 GARLIC CLOVE, FINELY CHOPPED

1 TABLESPOON FRESHLY CHOPPED FLAT-LEAF PARSLEY

1 EGG, BEATEN

SEA SALT AND FRESHLY GROUND BLACK PEPPER

These meatballs are made with a combination of beef and pork, but you could also use lamb (or veal) mince instead of pork. Use good-quality tinned tomatoes for a rich, tomatoey sauce.

1 To make the meatballs, soak the bread in the milk and leave for a few minutes. Put the minced meat in a large shallow dish or baking tray and add the onion, garlic, parsley and seasoning. Squeeze the excess milk from the bread and add to the mixture, along with the beaten egg.

2 Knead the mixture with clean hands for a couple of minutes until the ingredients are well combined (don't overwork it or the meatballs will become rubbery). Roll the mixture into small balls, about the size of a walnut, and place in a shallow roasting tin. The traditional way of cooking these is to fry them in batches in a little olive oil over a medium heat but I prefer to do it the easy way and roast them. Simply drizzle with a little olive oil (Spanish, if possible) and cook for 10 minutes in the oven at 180°C/ gas mark 4.

3 Meanwhile, make the sauce. Heat the oil in a large frying pan over a medium heat and add the onion, garlic and carrot and cook for a few minutes until the onion is translucent, but not coloured. Add the thyme, rosemary, salt and pepper, sugar and wine and flambé by setting light to the pan using a lighter or some long matches. (Flambéing is optional!) Simmer until the wine has reduced by half and then add the chopped tomatoes. Cook for a further 5 minutes, then add the peas and meatballs and cook together for another 15 minutes until the meatballs are cooked through. *Salud*!

NOTE

If your pan is too wide, the tomato sauce may evaporate too quickly and become dry. If this happens, just add a little water to the pan.

FOR THE SAUCE

5 TABLESPOONS GOOD-QUALITY OLIVE OIL

3/4 SPANISH ONION, FINELY CHOPPED

4 GARLIC CLOVES, FINELY CHOPPED

1 SMALL CARROT, PEELED AND FINELY CHOPPED

2 TABLESPOONS FRESHLY CHOPPED THYME

1 TABLESPOON FRESHLY CHOPPED ROSEMARY

1 TEASPOON SUGAR

1 GLASS OF SPANISH WHITE WINE

1 X 400-G TIN CHOPPED PLUM TOMATOES

HANDFUL OF FROZEN PEAS, DEFROSTED

SEA SALT AND FRESHLY GROUND BLACK PEPPER

MIGAS

FRIED BREAD WITH BACON, CHORIZO AND BLACK PUDDING

SERVES 4

PREPARATION TIME: 5 MINUTES, PLUS SOAKING

COOKING TIME: 15 MINUTES

400 G STALE SOURDOUGH BREAD

OLIVE OIL FOR FRYING

1 WHOLE HEAD OF GARLIC, CLOVES SEPARATED, SKINS ON

50 G PANCETA CURADA [CURED PORK BELLY] OR LARDONS

50 G MORCILLA [BLOOD SAUSAGE] OR BLACK PUDDING, THINLY SLICED [SEE NOTE]

50 G FRESH CHORIZO, ROUGHLY CHOPPED

1 TEASPOON SWEET PIMENTÓN

PINCH OF GROUND BLACK PEPPER

HANDFUL OF GRAPES

4 EGGS

Migas are simply cubes of bread fried in fat – this started life as a typical peasant dish. It can be made in a hundred different ways depending on the available ingredients. In this version the contrast of the flavoursome meats, with the silkiness of the egg yolk and the sweetness of the grapes is mind-blowing.

1 Trim away most of the outer crust of the bread loaf and cut the softer inside into 1-cm cubes. Sprinkle with cold water, cover with a damp cloth and leave for at least 30 minutes.

2 Place about 2 tablespoons of olive oil in a large pan over a high heat and start frying the garlic cloves. Add the chopped panceta curada and stir for about 2 minutes. Add the morcilla and chorizo and cook for 2 minutes. Squeeze out any moisture from the bread cubes, add to the pan and cook for 5 minutes, stirring constantly. Now add the sweet pimentón and pepper and set aside while you cook the eggs.

3 In a separate frying pan, fry the eggs (follow the instructions on page 69). Serve the eggs on top of the migas and top each plate with a few grapes.

NOTE

Morcilla is a type of blood sausage that is eaten throughout Spain, although obviously there are plenty of regional variations. I prefer to use Morcilla de Burgos but any good black pudding would do as well.

CARRILLERAS ESTOFADAS
BRAISED PORK CHEEKS

SERVES 4 AS A MAIN
PREPARATION TIME: 20 MINUTES
COOKING TIME: 2½–3½ HOURS

1 KG PORK OR BEEF CHEEKS

2 TEASPOONS OF SALT

2 TABLESPOONS FLOUR

100 ML OLIVE OIL

1 ONION, ROUGHLY CHOPPED

6 GARLIC CLOVES, PEELED

3 CARROTS, PEELED AND ROUGHLY CHOPPED

1 STICK CELERY, CHOPPED

2 BAY LEAVES

6 SPRIGS OF THYME

¼ CINNAMON STICK

1 CLOVE

5 BLACK PEPPERCORNS

3 TOMATOES, CHOPPED

175 ML PEDRO XIMÉNEZ SWEET SHERRY

175 ML RED WINE

1 BEEF STOCK CUBE

NOTE
You can substitute the cheeks with any other cut that is suitable for slow braising: shin, knuckle, skirt, flank, belly, ribs…

Pork cheeks are a sublime cut, lovely and tender when properly cooked; no bones, just delicious meat. I can't remember not having pork cheeks on the menu of my restaurants; the customers love them as much as I do. Some people say that marinating meat in red wine for 24 hours tenderizes it. I have done this literally hundreds of times but all I can say is that the meat tastes a bit more acidic and looks more purple. My suggestion is not to bother.

1 Season the cheeks with about half the salt and dust lightly with the flour.

2 Heat the olive oil in a large, heavy-based casserole over a high heat and add the pork cheeks. Pan-fry for about 3–4 minutes on each side. Remove from the pan and set aside.

3 Put the onion, garlic cloves, carrot and celery into the same pan and fry until dark golden, about 10 minutes. Add the bay leaves, thyme sprigs, dried spices and the chopped tomatoes and cook for about 5 minutes, until the juices from the tomatoes have reduced down.

Continued overleaf.

OMAR'S NOTE

If you are feeling lazy you
don't need to worry about
preparing any kind of side
dish to go with this: just
chuck some scrubbed new
potatoes into the pan for
the last hour of cooking.
They will cook beautifully
in the rich sauce.

4 Return the seared cheeks to the pan and
flambé: add the sherry and red wine and light
quickly using a lighter or long matches. Add
the remaining salt and when the liquid has
reduced by about two thirds, stir in the beef
stock cube along with 1 litre of water. Bring
to the boil and cook at a fast simmer for
30 minutes.

5 Reduce the heat to low and leave to simmer
gently for at least 2 hours – the cheeks may
need longer, even up to 3 hours, to become
really tender.

CORDERO DE CUENCO
ARAB-STYLE BRAISED LEG OF LAMB

SERVES 6

PREPARATION TIME: 20 MINUTES

COOKING TIME: 2 HOURS

2 ONIONS, FINELY CHOPPED

5 GARLIC CLOVES, THINLY SLICED

1 MANGO, PEAR, PEACH
OR PERSIMMON, PEELED
AND ROUGHLY CHOPPED

1 LEG OF LAMB,
APPROXIMATELY 2.5 KG

OLIVE OIL FOR DRIZZLING

2 TABLESPOONS
GOLDEN SULTANAS

HANDFUL OF DRIED PRUNES

HANDFUL OF SKINNED ALMONDS

PINCH OF SAFFRON

1 TABLESPOON HONEY

½ CINNAMON STICK

1 TEASPOON GROUND GINGER

4 SPRIGS OF THYME,
LEAVES PICKED

100 ML BRANDY

500 ML WATER

SALT AND FRESHLY
GROUND BLACK PEPPER

OMAR'S NOTE
This recipe is all about the prep and minimal cooking. The result is succulent and melting lamb with a rich and fruity sauce.

Spain today is still greatly influenced by its Arab heritage. The beauty of gastronomy as a cultural carrier is tangible and it always expresses a story. Each dish has a background, created from its surroundings. My friend Davinia showed me this very, very good and simple version once, and I've cooked it this way ever since.

1 Preheat the oven to 170°C/gas mark 3 and find a roasting tin, terracotta dish or similar that is big enough to hold all the ingredients comfortably.

2 Put the onion, garlic and chopped mango (or whichever fruit you are using) in the roasting tin and sit the leg of lamb on top. Season the lamb all over with salt and pepper and drizzle over some olive oil. Place in the preheated oven and cook for 1 hour.

3 Remove from the oven and lift out the leg of lamb. Add all the remaining ingredients and stir well until everything is mixed together. Put the lamb back in the roasting tin and return to the oven for a further 1 hour, or until the lamb is tender. Serve with rice or some good bread to mop up the delicious sauce.

JARRETES CON ALCACHOFAS

LAMB SHANK WITH ARTICHOKES

SERVES 2

PREPARATION TIME: 15 MINUTES

COOKING TIME: 3¼ HOURS

2 LAMB SHANKS

50 ML OLIVE OIL

5 GARLIC CLOVES, PEELED BUT LEFT WHOLE

½ SPANISH ONION, FINELY CHOPPED

1 CARROT, PEELED AND FINELY CHOPPED

1 CELERY STICK, FINELY CHOPPED

1 BAY LEAF

5 SAGE LEAVES

5 SPRIGS OF THYME OR 1 SPRIG OF ROSEMARY

1 TEASPOON TOMATO PURÉE

150 ML RED WINE

150 ML WHITE WINE

1 TEASPOON SUGAR

2 LARGE OR 4 SMALL GLOBE ARTICHOKES, PREPARED (SEE PAGE 122)

SALT AND FRESHLY GROUND BLACK PEPPER

This may take a while to cook but it is in fact very easy to prepare. This is one to make when you feel you deserve a treat – it definitely does the job. Prepare yourself for mellow, fall-off-the-bone lamb. If lamb is not your thing, you can always use shin or hock of beef. This dish is my idea of heaven.

1 Preheat the oven to 160°C/gas mark 3 and season the lamb shanks all over with salt and pepper.

2 Pour the oil into an ovenproof casserole dish; it needs to be big enough to hold both shanks tightly as well as the rest of the ingredients. Place it over a medium to high heat and add the lamb shanks. Brown them on all sides then remove from the pan and set aside.

3 Into the same oil add the whole garlic cloves, carrot, onion, celery and herbs. Cook for a few minutes until all the vegetables have acquired a dark brown colour. Add the tomato purée and cook for 1 minute before returning the lamb shanks to the pan. Add the red and white wine and simmer for 2 minutes until the wine has reduced.

4 Add the sugar, season with salt and pepper and add 1 litre of water. Bring to the boil, cover with a lid and cook in the oven for 3 hours, turning the shanks over two or three times during cooking so that no one part of the shank dries out. After 2½ hours, clean and prepare the artichokes (see page 122) and add them whole to the pan. They will cook to perfection in the last 30 minutes. After 3 hours the meat should be beautifully tender and falling off the bone.

5 If you like the rustic approach you can serve the dish pretty much as it is. If you want to go a step further you can remove the lamb and artichokes from the pan, skim the fat from the sauce and then strain the sauce into a clean pan. Reduce down until the sauce is very thick and sticky and then pour over the lamb and artichokes.

NOTE

The key for intense-tasting sauces when you are braising or slow-cooking any dish, is to brown and caramelize all the ingredients really well before you add any liquid to the pan.

LECHAZO ASADO

ROAST LAMB

SERVES 8

PREPARATION TIME: 5 MINUTES

COOKING TIME: 2¼–2½ HOURS

1 LARGE MILK-FED LAMB, ABOUT 5–6 KG, OR 2 SHOULDERS OF SPRING LAMB

100 G LARD (USE OLIVE OIL AS A LAST RESORT)

3 TABLESPOONS ROCK SALT

1 ONION, QUARTERED

4 GARLIC CLOVES, CRUSHED

1 BAY LEAF

200 ML WHITE WINE

1 BUNCH OF THYME

Throughout Castilla traditional shepherds have existed for centuries. Three particular sheep breeds (*churra*, *ojalada* and *castellana*) were celebrated for their flavour and these are the ones that have endured throughout the years. In Castilla this dish has to be prepared with a milk-fed lamb – the texture and flavour of an older animal simply doesn't compare. My family comes from Burgos in Castillay León and I have eaten this celebration dish all my life. It is traditionally cooked in baking houses, known as *asadores*, where the *lechazo*, or cooking of a whole milk-fed lamb, is the main event. The huge ovens here are wood-fired and have a special mechanism of a rotating stone base, which allows the chefs to turn the roasting trays inside the oven easily. Everyone should experience the *lechazo* at least once in their lives.

Let me show you how to replicate the wood-fired experience at home. Ask your butcher to source milk-fed lamb; alternatively you can use 2 shoulders from an older lamb and just cook them for longer.

1 Preheat the oven to 160°C/gas mark 3. Rub the lamb all over with the lard and rock salt and place it skin-side down on an oven rack.

2 Place the onion, garlic, bay leaf and white wine in a separate roasting tin and position the oven rack with the lamb on top of it (the roasting tin is only there to catch and flavour the dripping).

Place the bunch of thyme in a small flameproof, ovenproof dish in the bottom of the oven or somewhere where it won't come into contact with the lamb or the fat – the idea is to completely dry out the thyme. Cook for 1 hour 15 minutes.

3 Remove the lamb and roasting tin from the oven, turn the lamb over and spoon some of the juices in the tray over the skin. Add 1 glass of water to the juices so that there is some sauce by the end. Return to the oven. By now the thyme should be completely dry. Taking care not to burn the lamb or the sides of your oven, light the thyme sprigs using some long matches and quickly close the oven door. The lovely fragrant smoke will surround the lamb, creating the effect of a wood-fired oven. (You could also burn wooden skewers or toothpicks for this purpose). Roast the lamb, skin-side up, for another hour or until tender. If you are cooking shoulder, you will need to cook it for an extra hour or so.

4 Remove from the oven and allow to rest for 10–15 minutes before bringing to the table. Traditionally the lamb is cut into portions with the edge of a plate to show your guests how tender the meat has become. This is perfect served with panadera potatoes (see page 218) and the juices from the tray poured over.

NOTE
If your butcher cannot get hold of milk-fed lamb, make sure that it is young spring lamb.

COSTILLA DE CERDO A LA CERVEZA

BEER-BRAISED RIBS

SERVES 4 AS A MAIN DISH

PREPARATION TIME: 10 MINUTES

COOKING TIME: 1–1¼ HOURS

50 ML OLIVE OIL

1.5 KG PORK SPARE RIBS

1 SPANISH ONION,
ROUGHLY CHOPPED

5 GARLIC CLOVES, UNPEELED

100 G CHORIZO (FRESH OR
SEMI-DRIED), ROUGHLY CHOPPED

100 G PANCETA OR BACON,
ROUGHLY CHOPPED

1 TABLESPOON CLEAR HONEY

1 TEASPOON SWEET PIMENTÓN

1 BAY LEAF

4 SPRIGS OF THYME

2-3 POTATOES, PEELED
AND ROUGHLY CHOPPED

330 ML LAGER OF YOUR CHOICE

BREAD, TO SERVE

In Spain we like a good pig. It's a beloved animal, the one we do the most with. This recipe for beer-braised pork ribs is rich and hearty – we absolutely love it back home. I hope that once you cook it, you will understand why.

1 You can do this recipe in two different ways: either by cooking the whole dish in a large pan on the hob or by finishing it off by roasting it in the oven. If using the oven, preheat to 180°C/gas mark 4.

2 Put the olive oil into a roasting tray, a large terracotta pot or a heavy-based pan and place over a high heat. Add the ribs and pan-fry for about 5 minutes.

3 Add the onion, garlic cloves, chorizo and pancetta and cook for a few minutes until golden and starting to caramelize. Add the honey, pimentón, bay leaf, thyme and potatoes and cook, stirring, for a further 3 minutes.

4 Pour the beer into the tray or pan and either cook in the preheated oven for 1 hour or leave to simmer on the hob for about 45 minutes.

5 Serve these ribs with plenty of fresh bread to mop up the sauce and enjoy!

PINCHOS MORUNOS CON MOJO PICÓN

MOORISH SKEWERS

SERVES 4

PREPARATION TIME:
10 MINUTES, PLUS MARINATING

COOKING TIME: 5 MINUTES

500 G PORK FILLET (YOU CAN ALSO USE CHICKEN, BEEF OR LAMB, SEE NOTE OVERLEAF)

1 TEASPOON HOT OR SWEET PIMENTÓN

1 TEASPOON GROUND CUMIN

1 TEASPOON DRIED OREGANO

1 TABLESPOON FRESH THYME LEAVES

1 GARLIC CLOVE, FINELY CHOPPED

DRIZZLE OF OLIVE OIL

SALT AND FRESHLY GROUND BLACK PEPPER

FOR THE MOJO PICÓN

1 SLICE WHITE BREAD

4–5 TABLESPOONS SPANISH OLIVE OIL, PLUS EXTRA FOR FRYING

2 GARLIC CLOVES

5 DRIED CAYENNE CHILLIES

1 TEASPOON CUMIN SEEDS

1 TEASPOON SWEET PIMENTÓN

2 TEASPOONS SHERRY VINEGAR

SALT

These pork skewers with Moorish spices are an extremely popular tapa, although you could make them with any other meat. Mojo picón is a pepper sauce from the Canary Islands and is a fantastic accompaniment to meat, fish or potatoes. Picón means spicy, and you'll see why…

1 Trim the pork fillet of any excess fat and then cut into 2-cm cubes. Place the meat in a large mixing bowl and add the pimentón, cumin, some black pepper, oregano, thyme and garlic. Mix well, drizzle over the olive oil and leave to marinate for at least an hour, but anything up to 2 days is fine.

Continued overleaf.

OMAR'S NOTE

I absolutely love this marinade but there are times when I haven't got the energy or time for chopping, marinating or skewering. A quick alternative is to marinate a whole piece of beef and cook it like a large steak, either in a pan or on the barbecue. Simply let it rest for a few minutes after cooking and then slice into thick slices with a sharp knife. Fantastic results with about half the effort – what could be better?

2 Meanwhile, make the mojo picón. Start by frying the bread in a little olive oil, drain on kitchen paper and tear into pieces. Using a pestle and mortar, mash together the garlic, cayenne chillies, cumin seeds, pimentón, fried bread, vinegar and salt until you have a smooth paste. You could also use a food processor for this bit. Start adding the olive oil in a thin drizzle while you are still mixing.

3 When you are ready to cook the pinchos, thread the meat on to skewers (if you are using wooden skewers it's a good idea to soak them in water for 30 minutes to stop them burning). Pinchos morunos can be cooked over charcoal (the best way, in my opinion), under a hot grill or in a griddle pan over a very high heat. Cook for about 2 minutes on each side – you want them to be cooked through but still juicy on the inside. Season with salt and pepper and serve with the mojo picón.

NOTE
If you want to make these with chicken, use the thigh. If you are using beef use the skirt of flank and if you want to make lamb skewers use the leg.

CARNE GUISADA CON PATATAS

BEEF BRAISED WITH POTATOES

SERVES 5

PREPARATION TIME: 15 MINUTES

COOKING TIME: 2½ HOURS

1 KG STEWING BEEF, SUCH AS SHIN, WHICH IS VERY TENDER WHEN BRAISED

100 ML OLIVE OIL

2 ONIONS, THINLY SLICED

1 LONG THIN GREEN PEPPER, SEEDED AND THINLY SLICED

6-8 GARLIC CLOVES, THINLY SLICED

3 BAY LEAVES

4 SPRIGS OF THYME

10 WHOLE BLACK PEPPERCORNS

1 TABLESPOON PLAIN FLOUR

2 TABLESPOONS FRESHLY CHOPPED FLAT-LEAF PARSLEY

500 ML WHITE WINE OR DRY SHERRY

1 TABLESPOON VINEGAR (ANY KIND EXCEPT BALSAMIC)

500 G POTATOES, PEELED AND ROUGHLY CHOPPED

SALT AND FRESHLY GROUND BLACK PEPPER

If there is one dish that you will find in home kitchens throughout Spain, it has to be this one – beef braised with potatoes in white wine. It is quintessentially Spanish; no matter where you go, north, south, east or west you will smell the aroma of this dish being cooked. Very simple but also very good, in my opinion. My wife, on the other hand, thinks it's nothing too exciting. But the fact is, for any Spaniard, this comforting dish is the taste of home.

1 Cut your piece of stewing beef into 5 even-sized pieces and season with salt. Place a medium pan, just wide enough to hold all the ingredients, over a high heat and add the olive oil. Add the meat and brown on all sides until dark brown.

2 Add the onion, green pepper and garlic and cook for about 10 minutes or until the onion has acquired a dark golden colour. Add the bay leaves, thyme, black peppercorns, flour and finely chopped parsley and stir it all together for a minute so that the flour cooks.

3 Pour in the white wine or sherry and stir quickly to dissolve the flour evenly. Add the vinegar and let the liquid reduce by half before adding 500 ml water. Reduce the heat and simmer for 1½ hours before adding the chopped potatoes. Continue to cook for another 30 minutes, or until both the potatoes and beef are tender. Taste and adjust the seasoning and serve.

CIERVO AL CHOCOLATE

VENISON WITH CHOCOLATE

SERVES 3

PREPARATION TIME: 10 MINUTES

COOKING TIME: 25 MINUTES

1 SMALL BUNCH BABY
CARROTS, SCRUBBED

300 G VENISON LOIN

DRIZZLE OF CLEAR HONEY

1 TABLESPOON FRESHLY
CHOPPED FLAT-LEAF PARSLEY

SALT AND FRESHLY
GROUND BLACK PEPPER

FOR THE SAUCE

4 TABLESPOONS OLIVE OIL

2 GARLIC CLOVES, CRUSHED
BUT SKINS LEFT ON

1/4 SPANISH ONION,
FINELY CHOPPED

2 SPRIGS OF THYME

200 ML STOUT ALE

50 ML BEEF STOCK

2 PIECES (ABOUT 20 G)
DARK CHOCOLATE

SALT AND FRESHLY
GROUND BLACK PEPPER

Venison with chocolate might seem rather unusual but in fact this is a very simple dish to create.

1 Bring a large pan of salted water to the boil and cook the carrots in it for about 6 minutes, or until just cooked. Drain and set aside.

2 To make the sauce, heat 3 tablespoons of the oil in a separate pan over a medium heat and add the garlic cloves, onion and thyme sprigs. Cook for 5–6 minutes until the onions start to caramelize. Pour in the stout and beef stock to deglaze the pan and simmer until the liquid has reduced by half. Add the chocolate and seasoning and stir gently until the chocolate has melted. Pass the sauce through a sieve and keep warm while you cook the venison.

3 Season the venison loin with salt and pepper. Put the remaining oil in a pan over a medium to high heat and pan-fry the venison on all sides for about 7 minutes – it should be slightly pink in the middle but you can cook it for a little longer if you like. Remove from the pan and leave to rest for a few minutes.

4 While the venison is resting, sauté the carrots in the same pan to heat through. Add a drizzle of honey, the chopped parsley and season with salt.

5 To serve, slice the venison thickly and arrange the slices on top of the carrots. Spoon over the chocolate sauce.

RABO DE TORO
OXTAIL WITH RED WINE

SERVES 4 AS A MAIN

PREPARATION TIME: 15 MINUTES

COOKING TIME: 4½ HOURS

1 OXTAIL, ABOUT 2-3 KG

2 TABLESPOONS PLAIN FLOUR

100 ML OLIVE OIL

1 ONION, ROUGHLY CHOPPED

4 CARROTS, PEELED AND ROUGHLY CHOPPED

1 LEEK, ROUGHLY CHOPPED

5 GARLIC CLOVES, ROUGHLY CHOPPED

¼ CINNAMON STICK

1 CLOVE

5 BLACK PEPPERCORNS

4 TOMATOES, ROUGHLY CHOPPED

200 ML BRANDY

500 ML RED WINE

2 BAY LEAVES

2 SPRIGS OF ROSEMARY

SALT

SUGGESTION

For a change (it does change it quite a lot, actually) you can blend the sauce to make a great version of this toreros dish. Remove the oxtail, cinnamon stick and bay leaves before blending.

I love the less-prized cuts of any animal – you need to treat them skilfully to get the best out of them. I often find that the result is so satisfying that I keep coming back to it and this oxtail stew is no exception.

1 Trim away any excess fat from the oxtail and cut it into regular pieces through the bone. Season with salt and sprinkle with the flour, turning the pieces over so that they are evenly coated. Preheat the oven to 160°C/gas mark 3.

2 Heat the oil in a large, heavy-based casserole dish over a high heat. Brown the oxtail pieces on all sides, remove from the pan and set aside.

3 Add the onion, carrots, leek and garlic to the same pan and cook, stirring, for about 10 minutes or until they are fairly dark in colour. Then add the dried spices and chopped tomatoes and cook down for about 5 minutes.

4 Return the oxtail to the pan and give it a good stir. Pour the brandy and red wine into the pan and flambé quickly: use a lighter or long matches to set light to the alcohol. Cook until the liquid has reduced by half and then add the bay leaves and rosemary and about 2 litres of water. Reduce the heat to the lowest setting and leave to simmer on the hob for about 4 hours, half covered with a piece of baking parchment. Alternatively, cook in an oven preheated to 160°C/gas mark 3 for the same amount of time. The meat should be meltingly tender and the gravy will be dense and mellow.

VEGETABLES ★5

ESCALIVADA CON ROMESCO

ROASTED VEGETABLES WITH PEPPER AND NUT DIP

SERVES 4

PREPARATION TIME: 20 MINUTES

COOKING TIME: 40 MINUTES

FOR THE ESCALIVADA

3 RED PEPPERS

2 AUBERGINES

BUNCH OF SPRING ONIONS, TRIMMED

DRIZZLE OF OLIVE OIL

GENEROUS PINCH OF ROCK SALT

1 TABLESPOON SHERRY VINEGAR

Traditionally these roasted vegetables would be cooked over a charcoal grill – 'escalivar' means to cook in hot ashes. But, barbecues aside, not many of us have a charcoal grill at home so here's how to recreate this dish using an oven.

1 Start by roasting the vegetables for the dip. Place the red pepper, tomatoes and garlic head in a roasting tin, drizzle with a little oil and sprinkle with some salt. Place in a cold oven, turn the temperature to 200°C/gas mark 6 and roast for about 30 minutes.

2 Meanwhile, prepare the vegetables for the escalivada. If you have a gas hob, use tongs to hold the peppers and aubergines over the flame for a few minutes, turning them so that they start to blister all over. When they are nicely charred put them in a separate roasting tin with a drizzle of olive oil and some rock salt, then place in the oven. Char the spring onions in the same way and add them to the roasting pan after about 10 minutes, along with the almonds and hazelnuts for the dip (they are smaller and so take less time to cook). Roast for a further 10 minutes, then remove the nuts from the tin so that they don't continue to cook and burn.

3 Place the roasted vegetables in a container or shallow dish and cover tightly, ideally with clingfilm. This will make them much easier to peel. When cool enough to handle, peel away the skins and discard, along with the seeds from the peppers. Cut or break the peppers and aubergines into long strips and arrange in a serving dish with the spring onions and all the juices from the vegetables. Sprinkle over the sherry vinegar.

4 To make the romesco dip, peel the roasted vegetables, removing the seeds from the pepper and then just blend all of the ingredients together, using a hand blender, food processor or pestle and mortar. You should end up with a smooth paste. For a more refined texture, you can pass the sauce the sauce through a sieve.

5 Serve the roasted vegetables with the romesco dip on the side and let your guests take as much or as little as they want.

NOTE

Pimientos choriceros are Spanish dried peppers – they can be left out if you prefer. If you do get hold of them, you'll need to remove the seeds and stalk and then soak them in hot water. After 30 minutes, remove from the water and scrape the pulp from the inside (discarding the skin).

FOR THE ROMESCO DIP

1 RED PEPPER

3 TOMATOES

1/2 HEAD OF GARLIC

100 ML OLIVE OIL, PLUS EXTRA FOR DRIZZLING

PINCH OF ROCK SALT

50 G BLANCHED ALMONDS

30 G BLANCHED HAZELNUTS

3 TABLESPOONS SHERRY VINEGAR

PINCH OF SWEET PIMENTÓN

3 PIMIENTOS CHORICEROS, OPTIONAL (SEE NOTE)

GUISANTES CON JAMÓN

PEAS WITH SERRANO HAM AND EGGS

SERVES 3

PREPARATION TIME: 5 MINUTES

COOKING TIME: 10 MINUTES

250 G FROZEN PEAS

3 EGGS

4 GARLIC CLOVES, THINLY SLICED

1 GOOD DRIZZLE SPANISH OLIVE OIL

4 SLICES JAMÓN SERRANO
(CURED HAM), CHOPPED

2 TABLESPOONS DRY SHERRY,
SUCH AS AMONTILLADO

100 ML CHICKEN STOCK

FEW FRESH MINT LEAVES

SEA SALT AND FRESHLY GROUND
BLACK PEPPER

When people just boil peas and serve them with a knob of butter, it seems like a very boring part of a meal. To me, peas are better than caviar, full of flavour and sweetness. This recipe for peas with jamón serrano and a soft-boiled egg brings out the best in peas. Don't miss out.

1 Bring a large pan of salted water to the boil and add the frozen peas and eggs (wash them first) at the same time. Cook for no longer than 5 minutes. Don't worry that the water goes cold and it takes a while to come back to the boil, both the eggs and peas will cook to perfection. Drain in a colander and rinse the eggs under cold running water to cool down a little.

2 Meanwhile, place a large frying pan over a medium heat and add the sliced garlic and a drizzle of olive oil. After a minute, add the chopped jamón and fry quickly until it goes crisp (take care not to let the garlic go too brown). Add the sherry and then quickly light it with a lighter or some long matches to flambé the pan. Add the chicken stock, seasoning, fresh mint and drained peas and cook for 1 minute before transferring to warmed plates.

3 Peel the warm eggs carefully and cut in half – they should be quite soft, not hard-boiled. Place on top of the peas and sprinkle with a few flakes of sea salt. At this point I can't resist drizzling over a little more olive oil.

ALCACHOFAS Y ESPÁRRAGOS A LA GRANADINA

ARTICHOKES AND ASPARAGUS 'GRANADA' STYLE

SERVES 4 AS A TAPA
PREPARATION TIME: 15 MINUTES
COOKING TIME: 20 MINUTES

4 GLOBE ARTICHOKES

$1/2$ LEMON

1 BUNCH GREEN ASPARAGUS

50 ML OLIVE OIL

3 GARLIC CLOVES, THINLY SLICED

1 TABLESPOON PINE NUTS

PINCH OF CUMIN SEEDS

10 SAFFRON THREADS

1 TABLESPOON FRESHLY CHOPPED MINT

SPRIG OF THYME, LEAVES PICKED

40–50 ML WHITE WINE

SALT AND FRESHLY GROUND BLACK PEPPER

1 First prepare the artichokes. Trim the stalks and peel away the outer leaves so you are just left with the artichoke hearts. Scrape away any furry choke with a teaspoon and then run a lemon half over the hearts so they don't discolour. Trim the asparagus by peeling the bottom of the stalks and snapping off the hard ends.

2 Bring a large pan of salted water to the boil and squeeze the lemon half into it. Boil the artichokes for 10 minutes, adding the asparagus 2 minutes before the end of the cooking time. Drain and refresh under cold water.

3 Meanwhile, heat the oil in a frying pan over a medium heat and gently fry the sliced garlic and pine nuts until light golden. Add the cumin seeds and saffron and very quickly add the drained asparagus and artichokes. Sauté for a couple of minutes, adding the chopped mint, thyme leaves and seasoning as you toss the pan. Add the white wine and let it reduce until it has almost all evaporated.

OMAR'S NOTE

Replace the artichokes and asparagus with any of your favourite greens that are in season. That way you can eat this dish at its best, all year round.

ESPÁRRAGOS CON JAMÓN

ASPARAGUS WITH SERRANO HAM

SERVES 4 AS A TAPA

PREPARATION TIME: 10 MINUTES

COOKING TIME: 5 MINUTES

1 BUNCH GREEN ASPARAGUS, ABOUT 400 G

1 TABLESPOON OLIVE OIL

2 GARLIC CLOVES, THINLY SLICED

3 SLICES OF JAMÓN SERRANO (CURED HAM), ROUGHLY CHOPPED

2 TABLESPOONS DRY SHERRY

SPLASH OF SHERRY VINEGAR (OPTIONAL)

SEA SALT AND CRACKED BLACK PEPPER

MANCHEGO CHEESE AND JAMÓN SERRANO, TO SERVE

There's nothing better than fresh asparagus when it is in season. If you ever come across fresh Spanish white asparagus, buy it – but if it's from some far-flung corner of the world, don't bother – there are plenty of other things you can cook! White asparagus does need to be very fresh or it can be tough and bitter. If you do find white asparagus, just cook for an extra 10 minutes, adding a tablespoon of sugar and a knob of butter to the water.

1 Peel the ends of the asparagus spears or snap off and discard the ends. Drop the asparagus into a large pan of boiling salted water and blanch for 2 minutes. If you are using white asparagus, cook for longer (see above). Drain and refresh in cold water.

2 Heat the olive oil in a frying pan over a medium heat and add the garlic and jamón. Fry until golden and then add the blanched asparagus, season with salt and pepper and sauté for 30 seconds. Add the sherry and quickly flambé by setting light to the pan. Add the splash of sherry vinegar, if using, and serve with slices of Manchego cheese and jamón serrano.

OMAR'S NOTE
You can pretty much do this recipe with any fresh green vegetable that is in season – try mangetout, peas, green beans or broccoli.

PISTO
RATATOUILLE WITH FRIED EGGS

SERVES 4

PREPARATION TIME: 10 MINUTES

COOKING TIME: 25 MINUTES

4 TABLESPOONS OLIVE OIL, PLUS EXTRA FOR FRYING THE EGGS

1/2 SPANISH ONION, ROUGHLY CHOPPED

1 RED PEPPER, SEEDED AND DICED

4 GARLIC CLOVES, THINLY SLICED

1 SMALL AUBERGINE, DICED

1 COURGETTE, DICED

2 TOMATOES, DICED

PINCH OF SWEET SMOKED PIMENTÓN

PINCH OF GROUND CUMIN

4 EGGS

SEA SALT

This typical Spanish dish has as many variations as the country has regions. The variations are actually very different from each other, to the point that they should have different names. But, as with all the recipes in this book, here is my favourite version, similar to a ratatouille and usually served with fried eggs.

1 Heat the oil in a large frying pan over a high heat. Add the onion and cook for 2 minutes before adding the red pepper. Shake the pan and toss the vegetables as you cook them. After 2 minutes add the garlic and then after another 2 minutes add the aubergine. Cook for a further 2 minutes and then add the courgette. You are basically putting the softest vegetables in last so that they don't overcook.

2 Once the vegetables have started to caramelize, add the diced tomato, pimentón, cumin and salt and continue to cook for another 10 minutes, shaking the pan from time to time. Meanwhile fry the eggs (see page 69).

3 Serve the fried eggs on top of the pisto and sprinkle a little Maldon sea salt and some pimentón on the top.

PATATAS A LO POBRE
POOR MAN'S POTATOES

SERVES 4

PREPARATION TIME: 5 MINUTES

COOKING TIME: 20 MINUTES

1 LARGE SPANISH ONION, THINLY SLICED

4 MEDIUM POTATOES SUCH AS MARIS PIPER OR RED KING EDWARD, PEELED AND CUT INTO 1-CM SLICES

1 LARGE GREEN PEPPER, SEEDED AND THINLY SLICED

2 TABLESPOONS SHERRY VINEGAR

200 ML OLIVE OIL

SALT AND FRESHLY GROUND BLACK PEPPER

These are the perfect accompaniment to any meat or fish dish. (Pictured opposite.)

1 Mix together the onion, potatoes and pepper and season with the salt and pepper and vinegar.

2 Heat the olive oil in a large frying pan over a medium heat and add the onion, potato and pepper mixture. Cook for about 20 minutes, turning over occasionally. The vegetables should be soft, but not too crispy.

PATATAS CON ALIOLI
GARLIC MAYONNAISE POTATOES

SERVES 2 AS A TAPA

PREPARATION TIME: 5 MINUTES

COOKING TIME: 20–30 MINUTES

1 LARGE OR 2 MEDIUM POTATOES, SCRUBBED IN COLD WATER

1 BAY LEAF

2 TABLESPOONS SALT

2 TABLESPOONS ALIOLI [SEE PAGE 44]

1 TABLESPOON FRESHLY CHOPPED FLAT-LEAF PARSLEY OR CHIVES

1 Place the potatoes, bay leaf and salt in a large pot or pan and cover with cold water. Bring to the boil, reduce the heat and simmer for 20–30 minutes, depending on size. Use a small, sharp knife to check if they are cooked through.

2 Drain the potatoes and leave them to cool in their own time – do not be tempted to run them under cold water. Once they are cool enough to handle, use your fingers to peel off the skin. Quarter them lengthways and then cut each quarter into three or four pieces.

3 Place the potato chunks in a mixing bowl and add the alioli. Gently mix together and then top with the chopped parsley.

PAPAS ARRUGADAS CON MOJOS

WRINKLED POTATOES WITH MOJOS

SERVES 6 AS A TAPA
PREPARATION TIME: 10 MINUTES
COOKING TIME: 30 MINUTES

500 G NEW POTATOES
[IDEALLY ALL THE SAME SIZE],
SCRUBBED

4 TABLESPOONS ROCK SALT

FOR THE MOJO VERDE

3 GARLIC CLOVES

6 TABLESPOONS FRESHLY
CHOPPED CORIANDER

1 SMALL GREEN CHILLI
[OPTIONAL]

PINCH OF CUMIN SEEDS

SALT

1 TABLESPOON ANY VINEGAR
[EXCEPT BALSAMIC]

50 ML OLIVE OIL

FOR THE MOJO PICÓN

1 SLICE WHITE BREAD

4–5 TABLESPOONS SPANISH
OLIVE OIL, PLUS EXTRA
FOR FRYING

2 GARLIC CLOVES

5 DRIED CAYENNE CHILLIES

1 TEASPOON CUMIN SEEDS

1 TEASPOON SWEET PIMENTÓN

2 TEASPOONS SHERRY VINEGAR

SALT

This recipe is from the Canary Islands, where my mum and aunty lived for a good 10 years when they were children. Because of this, dishes from the Canary Islands pop up every now and then at my family gatherings, particularly at my aunty's house.

1 Put the potatoes in a large pot or pan, add just enough cold water to cover them and add the salt. I know it seems like a lot of salt, but trust me! Place over a high heat, bring to the boil and cook for 20 minutes or until soft (depending on the size).

2 Meanwhile make the mojos. You can do this the old-fashioned way, by pounding everything together with a pestle and mortar or by using a hand blender. If you are using a pestle and mortar start by grinding the dry ingredients first, then add the vinegar and then the oil in a steady stream, pounding as you go. This is so that the ingredients emulsify properly.

3 Use the lid of the pot or a plate to drain most of the water from the potatoes, retaining about a wine glassful. Place the potatoes (now with just a tiny bit of water) back on a low heat and reduce the water down while gently stirring the potatoes so that they don't catch. As the water evaporates a crust of salt should form on the bottom of the pot and surrounding the potatoes.

Continued overleaf.

Keep stirring the potatoes for a couple of minutes over a low heat until they start to wrinkle. Remove from the heat and let them rest for a few minutes before serving with the mojos.

NOTE
Both these mojo sauces are really versatile and can be used as a dip or sauce with many other dishes. It's traditional to use the mojo verde with fish dishes and the mojo picón with meat. Mojo picón will keep for several days in an airtight container in the fridge but mojo verde will only last a couple of days because of the fresh herbs.

PIMIENTOS RELLENOS DE BRANDADA DE BACALAO

PEPPERS STUFFED WITH COD IN WHITE SAUCE

SERVES 6 AS A TAPA

PREPARATION TIME: 10 MINUTES

COOKING TIME: 1 HOUR

FOR THE STUFFED PEPPERS

50 ML OLIVE OIL

2 GARLIC CLOVES,
FINELY CHOPPED

500 G FRESH COD FILLET,
CLEANED AND CUT INTO CHUNKS

GOOD PINCH OF SALT

50 ML DOUBLE CREAM

6 TINNED PIQUILLO PEPPERS

FOR THE WHITE SAUCE

50 ML OLIVE OIL

1 SMALL TABLESPOON FLOUR

200 ML MILK

4 TINNED PIQUILLO PEPPERS

SALT AND FRESHLY GROUND
BLACK PEPPER

This tapa is a real delicacy for me – I love the subtle flavours and textures.

1 Preheat the oven to 180°C/gas mark 4.

2 Start by making the white sauce. Put the olive oil and flour in a small pan over a medium heat and cook for about 5 minutes. Add the milk, seasoning and piquillo peppers and bring to the boil. Use a stick or hand blender to blend the sauce and return to the heat. Continue to cook for a further 20 minutes, giving it a stir every 5 minutes. It should be thick and creamy.

3 To make the stuffing for the peppers, put the olive oil in a small frying pan over a low heat and add the garlic. Cook for just 1 minute and then add the cod pieces, salt and cream. Cook very slowly on the lowest heat for about 20 minutes so that the cod starts to confit and release its own juices. You should have lots of oil and white juices in the pan, as well as flakes of cooked cod. Use a potato masher or fork to mash into a thick paste.

4 Use a spoon to fill the piquillo peppers with the brandada (cod mixture). Lay them in a roasting tin, cover with the white sauce and cook in the oven for 10 minutes.

TRINXAT DE LA CERDANYA

CABBAGE AND POTATO CAKES

SERVES 6 AS A TAPA

PREPARATION TIME: 5 MINUTES

COOKING TIME: 30 MINUTES

3 MEDIUM POTATOES,
ABOUT 300 G, PEELED

½ WINTER WHITE CABBAGE,
ABOUT 500 G, SLICED

50 ML OLIVE OIL

6 GARLIC CLOVES,
FINELY CHOPPED

6 SLICES PANCETA CURADA
OR STREAKY BACON

SALT AND FRESHLY GROUND
BLACK PEPPER

ALIOLI (SEE PAGE 44),
TO SERVE

These Catalonian potato and cabbage cakes with bacon and aioli are a real treat.

1 Slice the potatoes into 2-cm thick slices, place in a pan of salted water and bring to the boil. After 5 minutes add the sliced cabbage and cook for another 10–15 minutes, until the potatoes are soft. Drain thoroughly and return to the pan. Use a fork to mash the potatoes and cabbage together but don't over do it – you want to be able to differentiate between the potato and the cabbage.

2 Heat half the olive oil in a wide non-stick pan over a medium heat and add the garlic. When it is light golden pour it over the potato and cabbage mix. Season with salt and pepper and mix together.

3 Pour the remaining olive oil into the pan and place over a medium heat. Use a spoon to put scoops of the potato and cabbage mixture into the pan, flatten them slightly so you have a patty shape and then pan-fry for a few minutes on each side. Remove from the pan, drain on kitchen paper and set aside.

4 Quickly fry the bacon slices until crisp and then top each potato cake with a slice of bacon and a dollop of alioli.

NOTE

Savoy cabbage can work too but this is winter food and tastes better with white cabbage.

COCA DE RECAPTE

HERRING AND VEGETABLE TART

SERVES 6

PREPARATION TIME:
40 MINUTES, PLUS RESTING

COOKING TIME: 45 MINUTES

FOR THE DOUGH

20 G DRIED YEAST

230 ML WARM WATER

300 G STRONG WHITE
OR WHOLEMEAL FLOUR

3 G SALT

110 ML OLIVE OIL

FOR THE TOPPING

1 QUANTITY OF ESCALIVADA
ROASTED VEGETABLES
(SEE PAGE 118)

100 G FRESH OR TINNED
HERRINGS, SARDINES OR
WHITING, CLEANED AND
FILLETED IF FRESH

SALT AND FRESHLY GROUND
BLACK PEPPER

This Catalonian-style pizza is a great street food staple. It's very common to see this in people's hands at local fairs and parties. I always make this coca recipe with any leftovers from the escalivada recipe (see page 118) and top it with whatever I have at home: tuna in oil, chorizo, olives…

1 First make the dough. Place the yeast in a bowl with the warm water and stir until dissolved. Add the flour and salt and stir together. You will need to work it with your hands for 5–7 minutes. Cover and let it rest in a warm place for 1 hour. Add the olive oil and mix again for another 10 minutes – you may be getting frustrated at this point as the dough can be quite slippery, but you will get there! Let it rest, covered, for another hour.

2 Preheat the oven to 200°C/gas mark 6. Roll the dough out on a floured surface and place into an oiled baking tray, or one lined with greaseproof paper. Spread the escalivada vegetables on top and season generously with salt and pepper.

3 Arrange the fish fillets on top of the vegetables and bake in the oven for about 15 minutes or until the base is crisp and golden. Serve hot or at room temperature.

PIMIENTOS ASADOS
ROASTED RED PEPPERS

SERVES 6 AS A TAPA

PREPARATION TIME: 10 MINUTES, PLUS RESTING

COOKING TIME: 40 MINUTES

8 RED PEPPERS

150 ML OLIVE OIL

5 GARLIC CLOVES, THINLY SLICED

1 TEASPOON SUGAR

4 TABLESPOONS SHERRY VINEGAR

SALT AND FRESHLY GROUND BLACK PEPPER

It may sound strange but this simple tapa of roasted red peppers is one of the top three that my mum cooks and always reminds me of home whenever I eat it. It's one of my favourite and is best enjoyed with other dishes. Many years ago while working for Ferran Adriá, Ramón the head chef – and now a very good friend of mine – told me something I will never forget: fine dining does not mean building a complex dish with different flavours, garnishes and sauces; fine dining means that when you roast a pepper, you roast it to perfection.

1 Preheat the oven to 200°C/gas mark 6.

2 Place the peppers in a roasting tray, drizzle with some of the olive oil and sprinkle with salt, using your hands to rub them all over. Roast them in the oven for 25 minutes, turning them over halfway through the cooking time.

3 Remove from the oven; the skin of the peppers should be charred and blackened in places. Cover the entire tray in clingfilm and let them rest for 15 minutes; the steam will make them easier to peel. To peel them, first pull the stalk with the seed from the middle, keeping all the juices on the tray. Peel the skin away with your fingers and set the skinned peppers aside on a plate. Slice the peppers into strips; if they release more juice, add it to the juices in the tray.

4 Put the remaining olive oil in a wide frying pan over a medium to high heat and add the sliced garlic (you do not need to heat the oil first as you will be frying from cold). When the garlic is light golden add the pepper strips and sauté for a couple of minutes. Add the sugar and vinegar, season with salt and pepper, then sauté for a further 2 minutes. Strain all the saved juices from the skins and seeds into the pan and let them reduce for a further 5 minutes. If everything has gone right, you should have one of my favourite foods in front of you. *Buen provecho*!

SUGGESTION

If you are unfazed by peeling large amounts of peppers, triple the quantities, allow to cool and store in an airtight preserving jar; the peppers will keep for months.

SETAS AL AJILLO
MUSHROOMS WITH GARLIC

SERVES 3

PREPARATION TIME: 10 MINUTES

COOKING TIME: 10 MINUTES

300 G WILD MUSHROOMS,
SUCH AS OYSTER, OR A MIXTURE
OF WILD AND FIELD MUSHROOMS

8 TABLESPOONS OLIVE OIL

3 GARLIC CLOVES,
FINELY CHOPPED

1 TABLESPOON FRESHLY
CHOPPED FLAT-LEAF PARSLEY

3 SPRIGS OF FRESH THYME

SPLASH OF WHITE WINE

SEA SALT AND FRESHLY
GROUND BLACK PEPPER

Seasonal mushrooms with garlic. I have always been a big fan of mushrooms, as everyone in my family loves going to the forest and woodlands for trekking and mushroom picking is always part of the plan. This recipe can be adjusted to use any type of mushroom.

1 Trim the ends of the mushrooms and wipe them clean with a damp cloth. If they are particularly dirty, rinse carefully in cold water and dry quickly on kitchen paper, before they absorb too much water.

2 Heat the olive oil in a large frying pan and fry the mushrooms, insides facing up, for a couple of minutes. Season the insides with salt and pepper and flip over. Season again and fry for another 2 minutes. Add the chopped garlic and parsley and cook, stirring, for a couple of minutes.

3 Add the thyme sprigs and wine and set light to the pan with a lighter or some long matches. Let it flambé for about 30 seconds and then serve.

COCA DE CEBOLLA Y ANCHOAS

CARAMELIZED ONION AND ANCHOVY TART

SERVES 6

PREPARATION TIME: 30 MINUTES, PLUS RESTING

COOKING TIME: 30 MINUTES

1 QUANTITY OF COCA DOUGH
[SEE PAGE 133]

FOR THE TOPPING

100 G BUTTER

6 MEDIUM ONIONS, THINLY SLICED

40 G TINNED SALTED ANCHOVIES

3 TABLESPOONS PINE NUTS

Use Spanish salted anchovies for the topping as they will be of a much higher quality than anything else you will find.

1 Heat the butter in a large frying pan over a medium heat and add the onions. Cook, stirring occasionally, for as long as it takes them to caramelize and turn brown, about 1 hour. If they stick to the bottom of the pan and burn a little bit, that is absolutely fine, just add a tiny amount of water and deglaze the burnt bit. This technique will make the onions really sweet. People tend to add all sorts of things like sugar, salt, balsamic vinegar or red wine but at Ferran Adrià's restaurant we caramelized onions this way and I can tell you that after trying many other methods, this one is simply the best.

2 Preheat the oven to 200°C/gas mark 6.

3 Roll the prepared dough out to a thickness of 5 mm on a floured surface and transfer to an oiled baking tray. Spread over the caramelized onion and arrange the anchovies on top. Sprinkle with the pine nuts and bake in the oven for about 15 minutes, or until the base is crisp and golden. Enjoy!

ENSALADA DE HINOJO Y NARANJA

FENNEL AND ORANGE SALAD

SERVES 4

PREPARATION TIME: 10 MINUTES

2 ORANGES

HANDFUL OF PITTED BLACK OLIVES

1 SMALL COS OR
ROMAINE LETTUCE

1/4 RED ONION, FINELY SLICED

1 SMALL FENNEL BULB,
TRIMMED AND FINELY SLICED

1 TABLESPOON FRESHLY
CHOPPED OREGANO

SQUEEZE OF LEMON

GOOD LONG DRIZZLE OF OLIVE OIL

SALT AND FRESHLY GROUND
BLACK PEPPER

I grew up eating salad every day –
sometimes twice a day. Most of the time
it would just be a few leaves with whatever
ingredients were to hand at the time. As
you can imagine, that's quite a lot of salad.
After years of mixing and matching different
ingredients I've come up with hundreds of
salad combinations, but this fennel and
orange salad is the one I go back to again
and again.

1 Peel the oranges with a small sharp knife,
removing all the white pith as well. Slice
the oranges. Slice the olives if you wish –
you can also leave them whole.

2 Roughly chop the lettuce and arrange on
a serving dish and arrange the sliced onion,
fennel, orange slices and olives on top. Scatter
over the fresh oregano and dress with the
lemon juice, olive oil and salt and pepper.

EMPANADA GALLEGA

TUNA AND PEPPER FILLED PASTRY

SERVES 6

PREPARATION TIME: 30 MINUTES, PLUS RESTING

COOKING TIME: 1¼ HOURS

FOR THE DOUGH

15 G DRIED YEAST

250 ML WARM WATER

500 G STRONG FLOUR

1 TEASPOON SALT

100 ML OIL

1 EGG, BEATEN

FOR THE FILLING

100 ML OLIVE OIL

3 RED PEPPERS, SEEDED AND THINLY SLICED

2 ONIONS, THINLY SLICED

1 BAY LEAF

1 TEASPOON SWEET PIMENTÓN

2 TOMATOES, CHOPPED

200 ML WHITE WINE

2 EGGS

200 G TINNED TUNA IN OIL, DRAINED

PINCH OF SALT

In my restaurants I always take the time to talk to guests and obviously the conversation always turns to food and Spain. I love hearing other people's experiences of Spanish food. If anyone has ever been to Galicia they are sure to have tried this delicious filled pastry. This recipe is for all those of you who have tried it and long to eat it again, as well as those of you who have yet to discover it.

1 To make the dough dissolve the yeast in the warm water in a large bowl. Add the flour, salt and oil and mix well. Bring the dough together with your hands and knead for about 10 minutes. Leave to rest, covered, in a warm place for 1 hour.

2 Meanwhile make the filling. Heat the olive oil in a large frying pan over a medium heat and add the red peppers, onions and bay leaf. Cook for about 25 minutes, or until soft. Add the salt and pimentón and stir for 15 seconds before adding the chopped tomatoes. Cook for a further 3 minutes and then pour in the white wine. Simmer for about 10 minutes until the wine has reduced, remove and discard the bay leaf and set aside.

3 Hard-boil the eggs in boiling water for 8–10 minutes. Rinse under cold water and when cool enough to handle, peel and roughly chop. Add them to the peppers along with the drained tuna and mix gently.

4 Preheat the oven to 200°C/gas mark 6. Sprinkle a bit of flour on a flat surface and on your hands and use a rolling pin to roll out the dough to a thickness of no more than 5 mm – the thinner the better. It should be big enough to cover a baking tray when folded in half over the filling. Place in a lightly oiled baking tray and prick the surface of the dough with a fork.

5 Spread the filling over half of the rolled dough and fold the other half over it. Seal the edges, either by pressing round the edges with a fork or pinching together with your fingers. Make four small holes with your finger at each corner of the pastry so that the steam can escape during cooking. Brush all over with the beaten egg and bake in the oven for about 30 minutes or until golden and crisp. Allow to cool and serve at room temperature.

NOTE

For a vegetarian alternative, simply replace the tuna and eggs with spinach and cooked chickpeas.

LOMBARDA A LA MADRILEÑA

BRAISED RED CABBAGE WITH APPLES

SERVES 8

PREPARATION TIME: 10 MINUTES

COOKING TIME: 2–3 HOURS

50 ML OLIVE OIL

2 GARLIC CLOVES, THINLY SLICED

1 ONION, THINLY SLICED

1 RED CABBAGE, FINELY SHREDDED

2 SWEET RED APPLES, CORED AND ROUGHLY SLICED

8–10 TABLESPOONS SHERRY OR RED WINE VINEGAR

1 GENEROUS TEASPOON SALT

2 TABLESPOONS SUGAR

5 CRACKED BLACK PEPPERCORNS

1 CLOVE

In my family we eat this dish of braised red cabbage with apples as a starter on Christmas Eve. I was born and bred in Madrid and this is a very traditional Christmas dish; in fact I can't recall a Christmas without it. My great aunty Tere is always in charge of this dish but I am the one she gives it to to try first, to check whether it's missing something.

1 Heat the oil in a large pot over a low heat and start frying the garlic and onion. After 5 minutes add the remaining ingredients and stir well to combine.

2 Add enough water to cover and bring to the boil. Reduce the heat, cover and leave to simmer for 2–3 hours, stirring occasionally. The cooking time will depend on how soft you like it. The liquid should have reduced down to about half. Serve in a soup plate and eat with a spoon.

SUGGESTION

I like this dish exactly as it is but you could do what some families do and add a few raisins along with the other ingredients or scatter over a few toasted pine nuts before serving.

SOUPSANDSTEWS 6

GAZPACHO
CHILLED TOMATO AND PEPPER SOUP

SERVES 6

PREPARATION TIME: 20 MINUTES

8 TOMATOES, QUARTERED

1/2 SPANISH ONION, ROUGHLY CHOPPED

1 RED PEPPER, SEEDED AND CHOPPED

1 GREEN PEPPER, SEEDED AND CHOPPED

1 GARLIC CLOVE

1/4 CUCUMBER, CHOPPED

1 TEASPOON GROUND CUMIN

5 TABLESPOONS SHERRY VINEGAR

1 SLICE OF BREAD

1 GLASS WATER

10 TABLESPOONS SPANISH OLIVE OIL

SALT

ICE CUBES, CROUTONS AND OLIVE OIL, TO GARNISH

In summer you will find a bottle of gazpacho chilling in the fridge of pretty much every Spanish kitchen. I love mixing it up a bit – strawberries, raspberries, beetroot, cherries and watermelon are all things that have found their way into my gazpacho at one time or another. Try it, you will see what I mean!

1 Place all the prepared vegetables in a food processor or blender, reserving a little of the red and green pepper, cucumber and onion for the garnish. Add the cumin, sherry vinegar, bread, olive oil and about 200 ml of water. Add a pinch of salt and blend until smooth.

2 Check the seasoning and add more salt if necessary. If you don't like bits in your gazpacho you can pass through a sieve at this stage. Serve with a few ice cubes and garnish with the reserved pepper and cucumber, croutons and a few drops of olive oil.

NOTE

Gazpacho tastes so much better when prepared in advance – the night before if possible. If you do want to sieve it, I recommend you wait until just before serving as the flavour will be much more intense if it has been left overnight with all the bits in.

AJOBLANCO
CHILLED ALMOND SOUP

SERVES 6

PREPARATION TIME: 10 MINUTES

200 G SKINNED ALMONDS

150 G WHITE BREAD, CRUSTS REMOVED

1 GARLIC CLOVE

200 ML OLIVE OIL, PLUS EXTRA FOR DRIZZLING

3 TABLESPOONS SHERRY VINEGAR

600 ML WATER

1 TEASPOON SALT

FRESHLY GROUND BLACK PEPPER

HANDFUL OF GRAPES, TO SERVE

This chilled almond soup from the Malaga region is a phenomenal way to start a meal on a hot summer day. And, as with all cold Spanish soups, it's about as healthy as it gets.

1 Place all of the ingredients except the grapes in a bowl and chill in the fridge for at least a couple of hours so that the bread soaks up the liquid and it all gets really cold.

2 Transfer the contents of the bowl to a blender or use a stick blender to blitz until you have a completely smooth purée. The longer you blend it the smoother it will be but you may need to add a couple of ice cubes halfway through to keep it really chilled.

3 Serve in bowls with a few grapes on the top and a tiny drizzle of olive oil.

NOTE
To give the dish a special touch, blanch the grapes for about 30 seconds in boiling water, allow to cool and then peel before adding to the soup. You could also top the soup with fresh melon, apple or toasted flaked almonds instead of the grapes.

SOPA DE AJO

GARLIC SOUP

SERVES 4

PREPARATION TIME: 5 MINUTES

COOKING TIME: 15 MINUTES

100 ML OLIVE OIL

4 LARGE SLICES WHITE BREAD

7 GARLIC CLOVES, THINLY SLICED

100 G JAMÓN SERRANO
(CURED HAM), PANCETTA
OR BACON, CHOPPED

1 BAY LEAF

1 CHICKEN STOCK CUBE, CRUMBLED

1 TEASPOON SWEET PIMENTÓN

200 ML WHITE WINE

4 EGGS

SALT AND FRESHLY GROUND
BLACK PEPPER

There is nothing more comforting that a bowl of hot soup on a cold winter night. The problem with soups is that they often take a while to cook. This recipe is the answer to all your problems – it takes no longer than 15 minutes to prepare and scores high on satisfaction.

1 Heat a little of the olive oil in a large, wide pan and fry the bread on both sides until golden brown. Remove from the pan and set aside to cool. Chop into small cubes.

2 Add the remaining oil to the pan and fry the garlic and jamón until golden. Add the bay leaf, stock cube and pimentón and stir for 5 seconds before pouring in the white wine. Reduce for 2 minutes and then add 1 litre of water, the chopped bread and seasoning.

3 Bring to the boil and simmer for 10 minutes. Crack the eggs into the soup, give it a gentle stir (you want the eggs to stay unbroken) and bring back to the boil.

4 Serve piping hot in soup bowls.

NOTE

If you have individual heatproof soup bowls or terracotta dishes, you can serve the soup in them, break an egg into each one and bake in a hot oven for 5 minutes.

MARMITAKO
TUNA AND SAFFRON STEW

SERVES 4–6

PREPARATION TIME: 10 MINUTES

COOKING TIME: 40 MINUTES

3 TABLESPOONS OLIVE OIL

1/2 LARGE SPANISH ONION, FINELY CHOPPED

2 GARLIC CLOVES, FINELY CHOPPED

1 GREEN PEPPER, SEEDED AND FINELY CHOPPED

500 G POTATOES, PEELED AND ROUGHLY CHOPPED

1 RIPE TOMATO, CHOPPED

1 TEASPOON SWEET PIMENTÓN

5 SAFFRON THREADS

1/2 FISH STOCK CUBE OR, EVEN BETTER, 1 TEASPOON MISO SOUP POWDER

500 G FRESH TUNA, CUT INTO CHUNKS [SEE NOTE]

2 TABLESPOONS FRESHLY CHOPPED FLAT-LEAF PARSLEY

SALT

This tuna and potato stew is one of my favourites. It comes from the Basque country in northern Spain, from where, they say, the best food in the world comes. Traditionally this would be made with Spanish dried peppers called *pimientos choriceros*, but they can be hard to find outside Spain, so my version uses hot pimentón and saffron – the result is as good, if not better, my friends say.

1 Heat the olive oil in a pan over a medium heat and add the onion, garlic and pepper. Cook until softened, about 10 minutes. Add the potatoes, tomato and pimentón and cook for a further 5 minutes.

2 Add the saffron, 500 ml water and the fish stock cube or miso powder. Cook for about 15–20 minutes until the potatoes are done. Add the tuna and salt to taste. Remove from the heat (it will continue to cook with the heat from the water and potatoes), sprinkle with parsley and leave to stand for about 10 minutes before serving.

OMAR'S NOTE
Spanish tuna fishing is a tradition that goes back hundreds of years, when fishermen from the Basque country and Cantabria would sail out into the Bay of Biscay and use fishing rods to catch bonito tuna one by one. Bonito is a world apart from regular tuna – it has a rich flavour and soft texture. It is usually preserved in oil and can be found in jars in good super-markets and specialist food shops.

SUQUET DE PESCADO
CATALONIAN FISH STEW

SERVES 4

PREPARATION TIME: 25 MINUTES

COOKING TIME: 40 MINUTES

2 TABLESPOONS OLIVE OIL

4 X 150 G FILLETS OF MONKFISH, GROUPER OR HAKE, CUT INTO CHUNKS

400 G SEA BREAM OR RED SNAPPER FILLET, CUT INTO CHUNKS

1 ONION, FINELY CHOPPED

2 RIPE TOMATOES, CHOPPED

400 G POTATOES, OR 2 MEDIUM POTATOES, PEELED AND CUT INTO CHUNKS

1 LITRE WATER

½ FISH STOCK CUBE OR 1 TABLESPOON MISO POWDER

1 BAY LEAF

12–15 WHOLE MUSSELS, CLEANED [SEE PAGE 37]

8 PRAWNS OR LANGOUSTINES

FOR THE PICADA

100 ML OLIVE OIL

3 GARLIC CLOVES, CHOPPED

60 G ALMONDS, HAZELNUTS OR EVEN PINE NUTS

SPRIG OF FLAT-LEAF PARSLEY

PINCH OF SAFFRON

1 HEAPED TEASPOON SALT

This fish soup is a typical dish from the fishermen of the coast of Catalonia and Valencia, using whatever fish they hadn't managed to sell at the end of the day. Here's my own version using a selection of white fish.

1 First prepare the picada – an essential part of this dish which adds lots of flavour. Heat the oil in a pan over a medium heat and add the garlic and nuts. Fry until golden and then blend together with the oil, parsley, saffron and salt. You can do this in a food processor or blender or use a pestle and mortar. Process until you have a smooth paste; set aside.

2 Heat the olive oil in a large pan or casserole dish over a medium heat and fry the fish until just half cooked; this should take no more than 2 minutes for each fillet. Remove from the pan and set aside. Add the onion to the same pan and cook over a low heat until golden, then add the tomatoes. Cook for 5 minutes and then add the picada paste. Stir well and then add the potatoes. Cover with the water, add the stock cube or miso powder and bay leaf. Leave to simmer over a medium heat.

3 When the potatoes are about three-quarters cooked place the half-cooked fish, the mussels and prawns or langoustines into the pan and give it all a gentle shake to mix together. Simmer for a further 4 minutes, or until the mussels open and the fish is cooked.

CALDO GALLEGO
GALICIAN HOTPOT

SERVES 6

PREPARATION TIME: 15 MINUTES, PLUS SOAKING

COOKING TIME: 2½ HOURS

200 G DRIED WHITE BEANS

500 G CIME DI RAPA OR TURNIP TOPS [ASK YOUR GROCER, IF NOT YOU CAN USE CHARD, SAVOY CABBAGE OR CURLY KALE], ROUGHLY CHOPPED

100 G PORK LEAF LARD, ALSO CALLED KIDNEY'S FAT – ASK YOUR BUTCHER OR USE TOCINO [CURED PORK FAT] INSTEAD

1 FRESH CHORIZO

1 SALTED PORK BONE [WHATEVER THE BUTCHER HAS AVAILABLE]

500 G UNSMOKED GAMMON

4 POTATOES, PEELED AND CUT INTO 2-CM CUBES

SALT, TO SEASON

OMAR'S NOTE

If your caldo looks like it is drying out, simply add more water but always using boiling water, never cold.

Regional cooking is regional for a reason – it's about using ingredients available within our surrounding areas. Each plant or animal evolves to survive within a particular terrain, surviving against climates and predators. That is why recreating regional dishes can get a bit complicated. But don't let that put you off. This stew is worth the effort.

1 Soak the dried beans in cold water overnight.

2 To blanch the bitter turnip tops, place them in a large pan of cold water over a high heat. As the water starts to heat up give them a good stir and squeeze with your hands (as if you were washing clothes by hand) so they lose all the dirt and some of their bitterness. Let them boil for 2 minutes and then drain well. Plunge the turnip tops into fresh cold water to cool them down, drain and set aside.

3 Drain the soaked white beans and put into a large pan with all the meats and the bone and cover with 3 litres of cold water. Place over a high heat and when it comes to the boil, reduce to a slow simmer. Simmer for 2 hours, skimming the fat and scum from the top from time to time with a large spoon. Check the beans – if they are still hard, let it simmer for a bit longer.

4 Add the potatoes and the cooked turnip tops and let it all boil together for an extra 20 minutes. Check the seasoning. Serve in soup plates, making sure you divide up the meat so that each serving has a little bit of everything.

MENESTRA DE VERDURAS A LA NAVARRA

VEGETABLE STEW

SERVES 5

PREPARATION TIME: 15 MINUTES

COOKING TIME: 25 MINUTES

4 GLOBE ARTICHOKES

1 LEMON, HALVED

1 TABLESPOON SUGAR

1 BUNCH WHITE OR GREEN
ASPARAGUS (DEPENDING
ON THE SEASON), TRIMMED
AND CUT INTO 4-CM LENGTHS

1 CAULIFLOWER, CUT INTO FLORETS

2 CARROTS, PEELED AND SLICED

200 G GARDEN PEAS

200 G BABY BROAD BEANS

4 TABLESPOONS OLIVE OIL

5 GARLIC CLOVES, THINLY
SLICED

100 G JAMÓN SERRANO
(CURED HAM)

PINCH OF SWEET PIMENTÓN

1 TABLESPOON PLAIN FLOUR

1 TABLESPOON SALT

Not quite a soup, this dish is more of a stew, although it's as far from being a mush of overcooked vegetables as you could imagine. It's as flexible as the seasons – there's no need to stick exactly to the recipe, so substitute any vegetables with whatever is good and fresh.

1 To prepare the artichokes, trim the stalks and peel away the outer leaves so you are just left with the artichoke hearts. Scrape away any furry choke with a teaspoon, cut in half and then rub the hearts with a lemon half so they don't discolour.

2 Bring a large pan of water to the boil and add 1 teaspoon of salt, 1 teaspoon of the sugar and the juice of the other lemon half. Add the artichoke hearts and white asparagus, if using (white asparagus takes longer to cook). You need to add the vegetables in stages, depending on how long they will take to cook (the idea is to have all the vegetables cooked to perfection). After 5–6 minutes add the cauliflower florets, then after 3 minutes add the carrot and broad beans (if you are using green asparagus, add to the pan with the broad beans). Cook for 1–2 minutes and then add the peas and cook

for another 2 minutes. Drain in a colander, reserving about 400 ml of the hot vegetable stock. Refresh the vegetables under cold running water and drain again.

3 Heat the olive oil in a large, deep pan over a medium heat. Add the garlic and about half the jamón serrano, chopped. Once the garlic has turned light golden add the pimentón and flour and cook, stirring, for about 20 seconds. Pour in the reserved stock, a little at a time and stir vigorously to form a slightly thick sauce. Bring to the boil and then add the cooked vegetables. Simmer for 3 minutes to heat through, check the seasoning and serve with the remaining jamón serrano on top.

PATATAS A LA RIOJANA

POTATOES WITH PEPPERS AND CHORIZO

SERVES 6

PREPARATION TIME: 10 MINUTES

COOKING TIME: 44 MINUTES

100 ML OLIVE OIL

5 GARLIC CLOVES, THINLY SLICED

2 ONIONS, FINELY CHOPPED

2 RED PEPPERS, SEEDED
AND FINELY CHOPPED

3 TOMATOES, ROUGHLY CHOPPED

300 G SEMI-CURED CHORIZO,
CUT INTO 2-CM SLICES

½ TABLESPOON HOT PIMENTÓN
(OR USE SWEET PIMENTÓN AND
1 DRIED CAYENNE CHILLI)

1 KG FLOURY POTATOES,
PEELED AND CUT INTO CHUNKS

2 TABLESPOONS RED WINE
OR SHERRY VINEGAR

2 SPRIGS OF FRESH THYME,
LEAVES PICKED (OPTIONAL)

SALT AND FRESHLY GROUND
BLACK PEPPER

BREAD, TO SERVE

This chorizo and potato stew is rich in flavour and is the perfect comfort food. La Rioja, where the famous wine comes from, is an incredibly fertile area where some of the best fruit and vegetables in the Iberian Peninsula are grown (and that is a big statement). All these ingredients are traditionally from the region, hence the name.

1 Heat the olive oil in a large pan over a medium heat and add the garlic, onion and red pepper. Fry until golden, about 15 minutes.

2 Add the chopped tomatoes, chorizo, pimentón, potato chunks and cook for a further 5 minutes. Add the vinegar, thyme leaves (if using) and 1.5 litres of water. Season and bring to the boil. Simmer for about 25 minutes until the potatoes are cooked. Serve immediately with some good bread.

COCIDO MADRILEÑO

MADRID-STYLE STEW

SERVES 8

PREPARATION TIME: 30 MINUTES

COOKING TIME: 3 HOURS

1 BEEF MARROW BONE

1 TABLESPOON SALT

4 SMOKED CHORIZO SAUSAGES

1 SPANISH BLACK PUDDING
[OPTIONAL]

1 KG BEEF SHIN, BRISKET,
SILVERSIDE OR KNUCKLE

8 CHICKEN THIGHS OR LEGS

100 G TOCINO [DRIED PORK FAT] OR
SMOKED PANCETTA [NOT BACON]

2 CARROTS, PEELED

1 LARGE POTATO, PEELED

1 CELERY STALK

1 ONION, PEELED AND
STUDDED WITH 2 CLOVES

1 WINTER OR SAVOY CABBAGE,
QUARTERED LENGTHWAYS

1 BAY LEAF

500 G DRIED CHICKPEAS, SOAKED
OVERNIGHT IN COLD WATER

50 ML OLIVE OIL

4 GARLIC CLOVES, THINLY SLICED

200 G FIDEOS [THIN VERMICELLI]

Every Madrileño is immensely proud of this dish, but it has never yet been exported. Let's make it happen! Is this or is this not a Revolution? I should warn you, this is a time-consuming dish, but it's worth every minute of the effort. As with everything in life, when you get used to doing things they become effortless. But for a first-timer this should be a celebration dish, one that you cook for friends or family.

1 Before you start you need to understand that this is a hot pot with a lot of ingredients going in and a lot of ingredients coming out at different times. This ensures that each ingredient is cooked to perfection. Find the biggest pan or casserole dish you have and put in the marrow bones, salt, chorizo, black pudding (if using), beef shin, chicken thighs or legs, tocino, carrots, potato, celery, onion, cabbage and bay leaf.

2 Fill the pan with plenty of cold water. Place over a high heat and bring to the boil. Skim off any scum from the surface with a sieve or ladle. Tie the soaked chickpeas in a muslin cloth and add to the pot (so you can take them out later). Leave to simmer for 3 hours, skimming the surface every half hour or so.

3 Meanwhile prepare the dumplings. Mix together the garlic, parsley and bread. Add the eggs and 1 ladleful of the stock and mix to create a dough. Roll into small balls and set aside. Preheat the oven to 100°C/gas mark 2.

4 After 30 minutes of simmering, use a long spoon to remove the black pudding, carrots, potato, cabbage and celery and keep warm in the oven. After another 30 minutes, remove the chicken thighs or legs and transfer to the oven. Add the dumplings to the pan and cook in the broth for 30 minutes. Remove and set aside. Slice up the cooked cabbage and set aside.

5 Heat the oil in a separate pan and fry the sliced garlic until golden. Add the sliced, cooked cabbage and cook for 10 minutes, stirring all the time. Season with salt and set aside.

6 The chickpeas should take about 2 hours to cook but you can just remove the muslin bag and squeeze one chickpea between your fingers to see if it is soft or not. If you think they need longer, just return the muslin bag to the pan.

7 After 3 hours of cooking you should have a very rich broth with deliciously tender meats. Remove the shin, tocino, chorizo and marrow bones and set aside. Pass the broth through a sieve and place in a clean pan. Bring to the boil, add the fideos pasta and boil for just 1 minute.

8 Roughly slice the beef shin, tocino and chorizo and place on a large serving platter along with the marrow bones, black pudding and chicken thighs or legs. Slice the carrots, potatoes and celery and arrange on a separate platter with the dumplings, chickpeas and fried cabbage. Serve the broth with the pasta in a big soup bowl and let everyone help themselves.

Pictured overleaf.

FOR THE DUMPLINGS

3 GARLIC CLOVES, FINELY CHOPPED

1 TABLESPOONS FRESHLY CHOPPED FLAT-LEAF PARSLEY

6 SLICES BREAD, ROUGHLY TORN

2 EGGS

RICEANDPULSES ⭐7

PAELLA VALENCIANA

'THE' PAELLA

SERVES 6
PREPARATION TIME: 10 MINUTES
COOKING TIME: 55–60 MINUTES

1 G SAFFRON

1 TABLESPOON SALT

8 TABLESPOONS
SPANISH OLIVE OIL

400 G CHICKEN PIECES
(ON THE BONE)

400 G RABBIT PIECES
(ON THE BONE)

200 G RUNNER BEANS,
TRIMMED AND CUT INTO
2.5-CM PIECES

100 G BROAD BEANS OR
FRESH WHITE BUTTER BEANS

4 GARLIC CLOVES,
FINELY CHOPPED

1 LARGE OR 2 SMALL
TOMATOES, GRATED

½ TEASPOON SWEET PIMENTÓN

2 LITRES WATER OR LIGHT
CHICKEN STOCK

2–3 ARTICHOKES (DEPENDING
ON THE SIZE), CLEANED AND
TRIMMED (SEE PAGE 122)

500 G SPANISH RICE, SUCH
AS CALASPARRA OR BOMBA

1 SPRIG OF ROSEMARY

This famous Spanish dish is our equivalent of the Sunday roast, a dish that brings friends and family together. If the weather allows we cook it on an open fire – you are rewarded with an amazing smoky aroma. This paella recipe is the fruit both of my own investigations and those of top Valencian chefs and grandmothers. Follow this recipe and I guarantee you will soon be tasting the best paella. *Buen provecho*!

1 Wrap the saffron in foil and toast it for 30 seconds on each side in a paella pan over a medium heat. Remove from the pan and set aside.

2 Increase the heat to the maximum and season around the edges of the pan with the table salt. Wait until the pan is really hot and then drizzle with the olive oil. It should start smoking immediately; at this point throw in the pieces of chicken and rabbit (the meat needs to absorb the salt at this early stage). Fry the meat until nicely browned on all sides (this will add to the flavour of the paella).

3 Add the runner beans and broad beans and stir together for 1 minute before adding the garlic. Cook for 1 minute and then add the grated tomatoes (discarding the skin), pimentón and toasted saffron. Cook for 4 minutes, stirring all the time, until you can see that the tomatoes have lost most of the juice and changed colour.

Continued overleaf.

4 Add the water or chicken stock and leave to simmer for about 20 minutes, allowing the bits of caramelized chicken and vegetable on the bottom of the pan to dissolve so you get a rich stock. If you use chicken stock instead of water you will only need to simmer for 5 minutes. Check the seasoning but bear in mind that the rice will absorb a lot of saltiness, so it's okay if it tastes quite salty at this stage.

5 Cut the artichokes into quarters and add to the pan – if you add them any earlier the entire paella will turn dark in colour. Add the rice, spreading it evenly over the paella pan and stir just once. Cook on the highest heat for about 10–12 minutes before reducing the heat right down and cooking for a further 5–7 minutes. Once you have added the rice and given it a good stir you shouldn't touch the pan with a spoon again. You need to keep the film that develops on the top of the stock from breaking, otherwise the steam will escape and the rice won't cook evenly.

6 When the water is at a lower level than the rice itself, add the rosemary sprig. If the layer of rice on the top starts to look a bit crispy, cover the paella pan with a layer of newspaper for the last 5 minutes of cooking. This will help to steam the grains on top while the bottom gets crispy. In Spain this crispy bottom layer, the 'socarrat', is the most valuable part of the paella. Once the paella is finished it should look like a completely flat layer of rice. Leave to rest for 5 minutes before serving.

TIP
If you have some rice left in the paella pan, remove it to a plate otherwise it will take on a metallic taste.

If you want to make a good paella, you need to follow a few basic rules:

★ Use Spanish ingredients – they are just too good not to be used in this case. If you can, use saffron from La Mancha (it's the best in the world), Spanish olive oil and calasparra or bomba rice.

★ Get yourself a good paella pan – it should be wide and flat so that the rice cooks in a thin layer. Never use deep pans.

★ Never stir the rice. Ever! You will make the rice release starch and it will become too stodgy. At the end of the cooking time the rice should be light, soft and not sticky.

★ Let it rest for 5 minutes at the end of the cooking time. The rice should not be soupy so give it a chance to absorb any trapped steam.

★ Follow the recipe!

ARROZ CALDOSO CON BOGAVANTE

SOUPY LOBSTER RICE

SERVES 6

PREPARATION TIME: 30 MINUTES

COOKING TIME: 1¼ HOURS

2 LOBSTERS [FRESH OR FROZEN]

1 KG LARGE SHELL-ON
PRAWNS OR LANGOUSTINES

200 ML OLIVE OIL

1 TABLESPOON SALT

1 KG FRESH SQUID, CLEANED
AND ROUGHLY CHOPPED

1 RED AND 1 GREEN PEPPER,
SEEDED AND CHOPPED

10 GARLIC CLOVES,
FINELY CHOPPED

1 TEASPOON SWEET PIMENTÓN

1 G SAFFRON, TOASTED [SEE NOTE]

1 ÑORA DRIED PEPPER [OPTIONAL]

2 TOMATOES, GRATED OR CHOPPED

3 LITRES FISH STOCK
[SEE NEXT PAGE]

500 G BOMBA RICE

I think we can all agree that there is something quite marvellous about the delicate flavour and texture of the lobster. It is a shame it's so expensive and it's a real celebration ingredient. I so much enjoy eating this lavish, soupy rice… I urge you to experience it for yourself. Prepare yourself for a treat!

1 Start by making the stock. Peel the prawns and remove the heads. Remove the lobster claws and keep intact. Crack open the bodies to remove the tail meat and chop roughly. Set the peeled prawns, lobster tail meat and claws aside. Heat the oil in a large, wide pot and add the lobster and prawn shells and heads and brown for 5 minutes. Add the onion, carrot, leek, garlic cloves, bay leaf and peppercorns. Cook, stirring, for 10 minutes until golden. Add the chopped tomato and cook for 1 minute before adding the brandy and white wine. Boil for a couple of minutes so that the alcohol evaporates. Use a large spoon to squeeze the heads of the shellfish (to release all the juices) and then add 4 litres of hot water. Bring to the boil, skim the froth from the top and let it simmer for around 40 minutes.

2 Heat the olive oil in a large, wide pan and add the salt and chopped squid. The squid will release liquid that needs to evaporate before it can start frying and sticking to the bottom of the pan (this is what gives the dish its flavour). Take care as the hot squid can explode in the pan. When the squid starts to 'pop' add the chopped peppers and stir for 5 minutes. Then add the garlic and fry for 3 minutes. Follow with the pimentón, toasted saffron, crushed ñora (if using) and tomatoes and cook for 2–3 minutes until the tomatoes have reduced down a bit.

3 Strain the fish stock, add 3 litres to the pan and boil for 5 minutes before adding the rice. Cook over a high heat for 14 minutes, giving it a gentle stir every 5 minutes to make sure it's not burning on the bottom of the pan. Add the lobster claws, peeled prawns and chopped lobster tails to the pan and give it another gentle stir. Taste and adjust the seasoning. After a further 3 minutes, everything should be cooked to perfection.

4 The end dish should look yellowish from the saffron and pimentón, but slightly soupy and with lots of shellfish bits floating around. Serve in a soup plate and enjoy.

NOTE

Toasting saffron releases its glorious fragrance. Simply wrap the saffron in foil and use tongs to hold the parcel over an open flame on the hob for just 2 seconds on each side, flipping each side 5 times (10 seconds in total).

FOR THE STOCK

HEADS AND SHELLS OF THE PRAWNS AND LOBSTERS

100 ML OLIVE OIL

1 ONION, ROUGHLY CHOPPED

1 CARROT, PEELED AND CHOPPED

1 LEEK, ROUGHLY CHOPPED

1 HEAD OF GARLIC, CLOVES PEELED BUT LEFT WHOLE

1 BAY LEAF

4 BLACK PEPPERCORNS

1 TOMATO, CHOPPED

SPLASH OF BRANDY

200 ML WHITE WINE

ARROZ NEGRO MELOSO
SQUID INK RICE

SERVES 6
PREPARATION TIME: 30 MINUTES
COOKING TIME: 30 MINUTES

FOR THE STOCK

5 TABLESPOONS OLIVE OIL

PRAWN HEADS AND SHELLS
[SEE OPPOSITE]

1 LEEK, CHOPPED

1 WHOLE HEAD OF GARLIC,
SLICED IN HALF

2 TABLESPOONS BRANDY

200 ML WHITE WINE

TIP

I love to serve this rice with
a dollop of alioli (see page 44).

**To me this dish is the sea on a plate.
Made with prawns, squid and squid ink,
the striking, black ink-stained rice makes
the perfect special occasion dish. You don't
need much more than this for a complete
meal. This recipe is time-consuming and
needs a lot of stirring and love.**

1 First, make the stock. Heat the olive oil in
a large pot and fry the prawn heads and shells
over a high heat for a few minutes. Add the
chopped leek and head of garlic and continue
to cook for a few minutes until everything has
a good golden colour. Add the brandy and
quickly flambé by setting light to the pan with
a lighter or some long matches. Add the white
wine and cook until it has reduced by half, then
add 2.5 litres of water and bring back to the boil.
Boil for 10 minutes. Remove from the heat and
use a hand blender to purée until smooth. Pass
through a sieve and keep hot until needed.

2 Place a large, heavy-based pot or dish (a
deep paella pan is ideal) over the highest heat.
When it is searing hot, add the olive oil, salt
and squid – the squid will release a lot of liquid
which needs to evaporate. Once that happens it
will start frying and sticking to the bottom of
the pan. This part of the process is very important
as it will be pure concentrated flavour, but be
careful as the squid tends to explode! Keep
scraping the bottom of the pan to remove any
squid that is sticking so that it doesn't burn.

3 Once the squid is golden add the peppers
and onions and cook for 5 minutes until they
are golden brown. Add the garlic and after
a couple of minutes add the sweet pimentón

and saffron – keep stirring all the time as these two ingredients are very delicate and could burn in a matter of seconds. After 15 seconds add the squid ink and tomato and cook until the liquid has reduced by half.

4 Add the rice and stir through for a couple of minutes before adding the hot fish stock. Cook, stirring at all times, until the rice is tender and the liquid has been absorbed. This should take about 15–18 minutes but check the rice packet instructions. Keep stirring to stop the rice sticking and burning on the bottom and so that the rice develops a really nice consistency. Four minutes before the end of the cooking time, add the peeled prawns. Serve as soon as the rice is cooked – this dish waits for no man!

NOTE

Calasparra and bomba are varieties of short-grain rice that are perfect for this dish but they are not cheap. The reason Spanish rice is the most expensive is because it is the best. Well, I would say that, I know, but the reason it is the best is because it absorbs more water than any other type of rice in the world without losing its texture. The more stock the rice absorbs, the more flavour the dish will have. Paella isn't our most famous dish for nothing!

FOR THE RICE

150 ML OLIVE OIL

1 TABLESPOON SALT

1 KG FRESH SQUID OR CUTTLEFISH (0.6 KG PREPARED WEIGHT), CLEANED AND CHOPPED

1 RED AND 1 GREEN PEPPER, SEEDED AND FINELY CHOPPED

1/2 SPANISH ONION, FINELY CHOPPED

8 GARLIC CLOVES, FINELY CHOPPED

1 TEASPOON OF SWEET PIMENTÓN

PINCH OF SAFFRON STRANDS

5 SACHETS SQUID INK

2 TOMATOES, CHOPPED OR GRATED

500 G SPANISH RICE, SUCH AS CALASPARRA OR BOMBA (SEE NOTE)

2 LITRES HOT FISH STOCK

1 KG LARGE SHELL-ON PRAWNS, PEELED, HEADS AND SHELLS RESERVED

ARROZ CON COSTRA

BAKED RICE WITH A CRUST

SERVES 6

PREPARATION TIME: 15 MINUTES

COOKING TIME: 50 MINUTES, PLUS RESTING

100 ML OLIVE OIL

1 TEASPOON SALT

400 G BONELESS CHICKEN THIGHS, SKIN ON

300 G SAUSAGE, ROUGHLY CHOPPED

100 G PANCETTA OR CHORIZO, CUT INTO LARGE PIECES

4 GARLIC CLOVES, PEELED AND LEFT WHOLE

1 TEASPOON SWEET PIMENTÓN

PINCH OF SAFFRON

2 TOMATOES, GRATED

1 X 300-G TIN COOKED CHICKPEAS, DRAINED

1.5 LITRES CHICKEN STOCK

500 G BOMBA RICE

3 SPRIGS OF FRESH THYME, LEAVES PICKED

ZEST OF ½ LEMON

4 EGGS, BEATEN

This is another great Spanish rice dish from western Spain. It's essentially paella but with a delicious baked egg crust on the top.

1 First you need to find a wide ovenproof flameproof pan to cook the rice in – a 30-cm wide terracotta dish is ideal. Preheat the oven to 240°C/gas mark 9 (or the hottest it will go).

2 Pour the olive oil and salt into the pan and place over a high heat. Add the chicken pieces and cook until browned all over. Remove from the pan and set aside.

3 Add the sausage and pancetta to the pan with the garlic cloves and cook for a few minutes until caramelized and golden. Add the pimentón, saffron and tomatoes and cook for 3 minutes. Return the chicken to the pan, add the chickpeas and stock and bring to the boil.

4 Add the rice and thyme leaves to the pan and give it a gentle stir. If you stir the rice too much, it will release the starch and become gluey, and will also burn the rice on the bottom of the pan.

5 Mix the lemon zest with the eggs and add a pinch of salt. After 5 minutes of cooking the stock in the pan should be just above the level of the rice – at this point pour the egg mixture gently over the top of the rice, creating a layer of egg. Take off the heat and put the pan straight into the hot oven. After 10 minutes turn off the oven, open the door and let the rice rest inside the oven for a further 10 minutes before serving.

FIDEUÀ
PAELLA WITH PASTA

SERVES 2

PREPARATION TIME: 20 MINUTES

COOKING TIME: 30 MINUTES

150 ML OLIVE OIL

200 G FIDEOS [THIN, SHORT ANGEL HAIR PASTA] OR ANY ANGEL HAIR PASTA BROKEN INTO 2-CM LENGTHS

1 FRESH SQUID [ABOUT 350 G], CLEANED AND CHOPPED INTO 1-CM PIECES

10 PEELED PRAWNS, DEFROSTED IF FROZEN

2 GARLIC CLOVES, FINELY CHOPPED

1/4 SPANISH ONION, FINELY CHOPPED

1 TOMATO, FINELY CHOPPED

PINCH OF SAFFRON

1/2 TEASPOON SWEET PIMENTÓN

1/2 TEASPOON FISH STOCK POWDER OR CUBE

1 TEASPOON SALT

Fideuà is essentially paella made with pasta instead of rice. Like paella it should be cooked in a big paella pan so if you're cooking for large numbers it's almost impossible to cook paella in an average kitchen because of the size of the pan. The best way to cook paella is outside on an open fire. However, I promise you that this recipe works just fine in a normal frying pan, but only if you cook it for no more than three people, even better if you are just cooking for two. Although I'm a professional chef, I'm also a dedicated home cook so I know all the tricks and shortcuts.

This recipe is remarkably delicious, but it's also quick. If you do it properly, I've no doubt you will become as addicted to this recipe as I am.

1 Heat about one-third of the olive oil in a wide frying pan over a medium heat. Add the dried pasta and fry for about 5 minutes, or until it turns golden. Remove from the pan and set aside.

2 Add the rest of the olive oil to the pan, increase the heat and add the chopped squid and salt. Squid can be very temperamental as it releases a lot of water when you start cooking it so it tends to explode in the pan. It's fair to say this bit is a tiny bit dangerous. I recommend you hold a pan lid over the pan, so that the steam can still escape, and stand back. Give it a quick stir, half cover with the lid and leave to cook for a couple more minutes. Don't scrape the bottom of the pan, as that sticky layer on the bottom is essential for making a rich stock.

Continued overleaf.

3 When the squid has browned, add the peeled prawns, garlic and onion and cook for another 5 minutes until everything is dark golden (this will happen fairly quickly because of the high heat). Add the chopped tomato, saffron and pimentón and stir constantly to dissolve the sticky bits on the bottom. This should take no longer than 2 minutes.

4 Add the fish stock powder or cube and 1 litre of water. Bring to the boil and let it simmer for about 10 minutes before adding the fried pasta. You need to use your judgement here – you need just enough water left in the pan for the pasta to cook and absorb all the remaining liquid. A good thin fideo pasta should cook in about 3 minutes. Stir in the pasta, cover the pan and cook until the liquid has been absorbed.

5 Remove from the heat and leave for 1 more minute, uncovered, to create a toasted layer of pasta on the bottom of the pan – it will taste like heaven. Enjoy with a good dollop of alioli (see page 44).

ARROZ MELOSO DE VERDURAS

MELLOW VEGETABLE RICE

SERVES 5

PREPARATION TIME: 20 MINUTES

COOKING TIME: 1 HOUR

150 ML OLIVE OIL

1 TEASPOON SALT

1 ONION, CHOPPED

1 RED PEPPER, SEEDED AND CHOPPED

1 SMALL FENNEL BULB, CHOPPED

HANDFUL OF GREEN BEANS, HALVED OR SLICED

1 COURGETTE, CHOPPED

6 GARLIC CLOVES, SLICED

1 TEASPOON SWEET PIMENTÓN

1 G SAFFRON, TOASTED [SEE PAGE 169]

1 DRIED OR FRESH RED CHILLI, SEEDED AND CHOPPED

2 TOMATOES, GRATED

1.5 LITRES VEGETABLE STOCK

3 ARTICHOKE HEARTS, QUARTERED [SEE PAGE 122]

350 G BOMBA RICE

3 SPRIGS OF FLAT-LEAF PARSLEY, LEAVES FINELY CHOPPED

OMAR'S NOTE

You wait for the rice, the rice doesn't wait for you.

1 Use a wide paella pan, or a wide-bottomed pan for this dish. Place it over a high heat and add the olive oil and salt. Add the onion, pepper and fennel and cook for a few minutes until golden, then add the beans, courgette and garlic. Cook each vegetable for a minute or two before adding the next one.

2 Add the pimentón, toasted saffron, chilli and tomatoes. Cook for 3 minutes and then add the stock. Bring it to the boil and add the artichokes and rice. Give it a good stir and leave to cook over a high heat for 10 minutes.

3 After 10 minutes add the chopped parsley leaves and then taste and adjust the seasoning. Reduce the heat to low, give it a final stir and leave the rice to cook for 5 minutes – without stirring. Remove from the heat and rest for a further 5 minutes before serving. Serve immediately – it should be eaten as soon as it's ready otherwise it will overcook.

ARROZ A LA AMPURDANESA

RICE WITH SAUSAGE AND RABBIT

SERVES 6

PREPARATION TIME: 30 MINUTES

COOKING TIME: 1 HOUR

100 ML OLIVE OIL

5 GARLIC CLOVES,
PEELED AND LEFT WHOLE

50 G ALMONDS, SKINNED
OR UNSKINNED

1 G SAFFRON

5 SPRIGS OF FRESH THYME,
LEAVES PICKED

2 TOMATOES, CHOPPED

1 RABBIT, SKINNED AND CUT INTO
PIECES BUT LEFT ON THE BONE

400 G WHITE SAUSAGE
(IN SPAIN WE WOULD USE
CATALONIAN BUTIFARRA)

1 ONION, FINELY CHOPPED

200 G WILD MUSHROOMS,
SUCH AS OYSTER, GIROLLE
OR RED PINE, CLEANED

500 G SPANISH RICE, SUCH
AS CALASPARRA OR BOMBA

1 TABLESPOON SALT

This rice dish from Catalonia was one of the first dishes I learned on the traditional Spanish cookery course I did at the age of 16 and it is still a favourite. Ideally use a large ovenproof terracotta or clay pot.

1 Heat the olive oil in a large ovenproof casserole dish or pan (ideally a terracotta dish). Add the garlic cloves and almonds and fry for a couple of minutes until golden. Remove from the pan and blend with the saffron, thyme and tomatoes, using a pestle and mortar or stick blender, until you have a smooth purée. Set aside.

2 Season the rabbit pieces all over with salt and add to the pan with the white sausage. Fry over a high heat until dark golden, then add the onion and cook, stirring for 5 minutes. Cut any large mushrooms into pieces and add to the pan and sauté for a further 5 minutes.

3 By now the meat and onion should be fairly brown. Add the blended paste and cook, stirring, for 3–4 minutes; then add 1.5 litres of water. Bring to the boil and simmer for 20 minutes until you have a rich stock. Meanwhile preheat the oven to 220°C/gas mark 7.

4 Add the rice to the pan and let it cook for about 10 minutes before putting the whole pan in the oven for a further 8 minutes. At the end of the cooking time turn the oven off, open the door and leave the pan to rest for 5 minutes in the oven before serving.

LENTEJAS ESTOFADAS

LENTIL STEW

SERVES 4

PREPARATION TIME: 20 MINUTES

COOKING TIME: 1 HOUR

5 TABLESPOONS OLIVE OIL

5 GARLIC CLOVES, UNPEELED

1/2 SPANISH ONION, FINELY CHOPPED

1 CARROT, PEELED AND DICED

1 STICK CELERY, FINELY CHOPPED

200 G FRESH OR COOKING CHORIZO (SMOKED IF POSSIBLE), DICED

100 G SMOKED PANCETA CURADA (CURED PORK BELLY) OR SMOKED BACON

1 BAY LEAF

2 TABLESPOONS FRESH THYME LEAVES

1 TEASPOON CUMIN SEEDS OR GROUND CUMIN

1 CLOVE

1 TEASPOON OF SWEET PIMENTÓN

100 ML RED WINE

200 G PARDINA OR PUY LENTILS

1 GOOD-QUALITY CHICKEN STOCK CUBE

SALT AND FRESHLY GROUND BLACK PEPPER

NOTE

In Spain we would add a ham bone – or even a morcilla de Burgos – to the lentils to intensify the flavour.

This recipe for braised lentils is real comfort food. It has a bit of everything – a warming liquid, flavoursome meats and healthy vegetables. Pulses are big in Spain and there are several varieties but to me, pardina lentils, with their distinct nutty flavour, are the best. If you can't get hold of them, use puy lentils.

1 Heat the olive oil in a large pan over a medium heat and add the garlic cloves. Add the onion, carrot and celery and cook for about 7 minutes or until the onion is light golden. Then add the chorizo, panceta curada, bay leaf, thyme, salt, pepper, cumin seeds and clove. Cook for 5 minutes, stirring occasionally, and then add the pimentón. Stir quickly so that it doesn't burn.

2 Pour in the red wine and cook until the liquid has all but evaporated. Now add 1 litre of cold water, the stock cube and the lentils (always add lentils to cold, not boiling, water or they will not cook properly).

3 Bring to the boil and leave to simmer for about 40 minutes or until the lentils are tender (there is nothing worse than undercooked lentils). Season with salt and pepper and enjoy.

FABADA ASTURIANA
ASTURIAN BEAN STEW

SERVES 4

PREPARATION TIME: 5 MINUTES

COOKING TIME: 3 HOURS

500 G FABES BEANS, OR
LARGE BUTTER BEANS, SOAKED
OVERNIGHT IN COLD WATER

200 G SMOKED AND AIR-DRIED
PANCETA (PORK BELLY), SOAKED
OVERNIGHT IN COLD WATER

300 G LACON (CURED PORK,
HAM HOCK OR KNUCKLE) OR
SMOKED GAMMON, SOAKED
OVERNIGHT IN COLD WATER

2 HEAVILY SMOKED CHORIZO
SAUSAGES

2 HEAVILY SMOKED MORCILLA
(BLACK PUDDING) SAUSAGES

PINCH OF SAFFRON

1 ONION, PEELED AND LEFT WHOLE

1 GARLIC CLOVE,
CRUSHED WITH SKIN ON

This cured meat and white bean stew must be one of Spain's most famous dishes and yet it is one of the most simple. The key to this recipe is the ingredients, which need to be from Asturias (otherwise it just won't be the same). Fabes are fat, white beans which cook beautifully without disintegrating – if you can't get hold of them you could use large lima beans or butter beans – but don't say that I said so...

1 Drain the beans and meat and place in a large, heavy-based pan or casserole dish along with all the remaining ingredients. Cover with cold water, approximately 3 litres, and place over a high heat.

2 As the liquid starts to come to the boil, scum will start to form on the surface; skim it away using a spoon or sieve. Skim any fat from the surface as well.

3 When the water starts to boil, add a long drizzle of cold water to the pan – this is to stop the skin of the beans from splitting. Repeat this technique twice more and then leave to simmer for about 3 hours, skimming the surface from time to time to remove any impurities.

4 After 3 hours you should have a thick, flavoursome bean stew. If the liquid does not look thick, remove the onion and blend with a little of the cooking liquid before returning to the pan. If you need to add more liquid to the pan during cooking, add boiling water, not cold.

5 To serve, chop the meats into pieces, give it a good stir and serve the stew in big bowls.

DESSERTS AND SWEET THINGS

★ 8

TORRIJAS DE MI MADRE
MUM'S EGGY BREAD

SERVES 6

PREPARATION TIME: 5 MINUTES, PLUS INFUSING AND CHILLING

COOKING TIME: 10 MINUTES

2 LITRES MILK

300 G SUGAR

1 CINNAMON STICK

1 LOAF DAY-OLD WHITE BREAD

VEGETABLE OIL OR MILD OLIVE OIL FOR FRYING

2 EGGS, BEATEN

FOR THE CINNAMON COATING

100 G SUGAR

1 TABLESPOON GROUND CINNAMON

SUGGESTION

Another way of serving these is with a sticky wine syrup. You'll need a bottle of good red wine – Spanish if possible – nothing too expensive. Place in a large pan with 200 g of sugar, 1 star anise and 1 cinnamon stick and bring to the boil. Reduce the heat and simmer for 10 minutes. Pour the wine syrup over just-cooked torrijas and leave to cool before eating.

This Spanish bread-and-butter pudding, usually made for Easter, is the one dish that really reminds me of my mum. She makes the best torrijas in the world – no contest.

1 Place the milk, sugar and cinnamon stick in a pan and bring almost to boiling point, stirring occasionally to dissolve the sugar. Remove from the heat and leave for about 15 minutes so the milk is infused with the cinnamon aroma.

2 Cut the bread into slices about 2–3 cm thick. Place the bread slices in a large shallow dish and pour the milk over. Chill for at least 2 hours, turning the slices over halfway through.

3 Heat the oil in a large frying pan over a medium heat – you need to be able to fry at least two slices of bread at a time. You could use butter instead of vegetable or olive oil but it's best avoided and will burn more quickly. When the oil is hot, quickly dip each slice of bread in the beaten egg so that it is fully coated, and then place in the hot oil. Take care – I've burnt my fingers too many times. After a couple of minutes, flip them over and fry them for another minute or two until golden. Remove from the pan and drain on kitchen paper.

4 Mix together the sugar and ground cinnamon and sprinkle it on both sides of the torrijas. Do this while they are still hot – the sugary coating will stick more easily. Breathe in the lovely warm aroma of cinnamon and enjoy!

BUÑUELOS DE VIENTO
CUSTARD-FILLED PUFFS

SERVES 10

PREPARATION TIME: 5 MINUTES

COOKING TIME: 10 MINUTES

100 ML WATER

45 G BUTTER

2 G TABLE SALT

75 G PLAIN FLOUR

2 LARGE EGGS

3 G BICARBONATE OF SODA

VEGETABLE OIL FOR FRYING

CASTER OR ICING SUGAR FOR DUSTING

WHIPPED CREAM FOR FILLING (OPTIONAL)

These light-as-air fritters (literally 'puffs of wind') shouldn't take you more than 15 minutes to prepare from beginning to end. You will see these sold from stalls on the streets of Madrid for All Saints Day. Sweets were not really for everyday eating so they evolved as something people ate to celebrate saints' days or special occasions. Another reason is because the nuns in the convents used to receive egg yolks from the nearby landlords of the vineyards who used egg whites to clarify the wine. The nuns invented ways to use up the excess egg yolks…!

1 Place the water, butter and salt in a pan and bring to the boil. Add the flour, remove from the heat and mix with a spoon for about 1 minute until it is well combined and the mixture has become a ball. Leave to rest for 5 minutes.

2 Add the eggs, one at a time. Mix into the dough until completely blended before adding the next one. Add the bicarbonate of soda and stir in – the mixture should have the consistency of thick yoghurt.

3 Pour enough oil into a deep pan to give you three fingers' depth of oil. Heat until a cube of day-old bread dropped in the oil turns golden in about 30 seconds. Alternatively heat a deep fryer to 190°C.

4 Use a couple of teaspoons to start dropping in knobs of dough, about the size of a cherry. The dough should start frying and puff up after about 30 seconds, and then they will turn over by themselves. Leave them in the oil until they turn golden brown, about 2 minutes. Scoop out with a slotted spoon and drain on kitchen paper. They should have a delicate crispness on the outside and be pretty much all air on the inside.

5 Dust with caster or icing sugar while still warm. If you want to fill with whipped cream, make a little cut on the side of each one and use a piping bag to fill.

SUGGESTION
You could also try filling these with chocolate ganache or custard.

EL FLAN DE MI MADRE

'THE' CRÈME CARAMEL

SERVES 5

PREPARATION TIME: 5 MINUTES

COOKING TIME: 1 HOUR

3 EGGS

1 X 400-G TIN CONDENSED MILK

700 ML FULL-FAT MILK

1 TABLESPOON VANILLA EXTRACT

FOR THE CARAMEL

2 TABLESPOONS SUGAR

1 TABLESPOON WATER

I have probably tasted around 60 different crème caramels in my life but I have never tasted one as good as the one my mum makes. And I am not saying this because it's my mum's – if I genuinely had tasted a better flan I would have put it in the book instead. One of my earliest memories is of Mum making this flan and, if that's not enough, this is the first thing I ever cooked – when I was just 4½ years old.

1 Preheat the oven to 180°C/gas mark 4. Find a deep-sided oval pie dish and half fill with water – this will be your bain marie.

2 To make the caramel, place the sugar and water into an ovenproof dish and place over a high heat until it starts to turn into a golden caramel. Using a cloth or oven gloves, swirl the caramel around the dish so that it covers the bottom and comes a little up the sides of the dish.

3 Whisk the eggs, condensed milk, milk and vanilla extract together using an electric whisk or blender (yes, it really is that simple). Pour this egg mixture into the caramelized dish and cover with foil. Place it into the bain marie and transfer to the oven.

4 Cook in the oven for 1 hour, remove from the oven and allow to cool before removing the foil. Place a plate over the top, flip over and remove the mould. The caramel should run down the sides of the flan. I hope is the best crème caramel you have ever tasted. If it's not, complaints to my mum, please!

TOCINILLO DE CIELO
FAT FROM HEAVEN

SERVES 4

PREPARATION TIME: 10 MINUTES

COOKING TIME: 30 MINUTES, PLUS CHILLING

130 G SUGAR

50 ML WATER

STRIP OF LEMON ZEST

4 EGG YOLKS

1 EGG

FOR THE CARAMEL

2 TABLESPOONS SUGAR

2 TABLESPOONS WATER

1 Find a small ovenproof dish for this dessert – it's very sweet so you only make it in small quantities. Put the sugar and water for the caramel into the dish and place over a medium heat until it turns to caramel and is a lovely golden colour. Swirl the caramel all over the bottom of the dish and a little up the sides. Set aside.

2 Put the sugar, water and lemon zest into a small pan over a medium heat. When it comes to the boil, let it bubble for a further 3 minutes. Take off the heat and remove and discard the lemon zest. Set aside for 5 minutes.

3 Very gently whisk together the egg yolks with the whole egg – you do not want to create any froth. Pour the warm syrup into the egg mixture in a thin, steady stream, whisking as you do so. Keep whisking until it is completely incorporated. Pour this mixture into the caramel-coated dish and place the dish inside a deep-sided roasting tin. Pour in a couple of fingers' depth of cold water (to create a bain marie) and put the whole thing in a cold oven. Turn the temperature to 160°C/gas mark 3 and cook for 25 minutes or until set. Take care not to overcook – it should still have a slight wobble.

4 Chill in the fridge for a couple of hours before serving. Run the point of a knife around the edge of the dish and then turn out on to a plate. Do not eat too much of this as it is extremely calorific, but it is a real treat.

CREMA CATALANA
CATALONIAN CUSTARD POTS

SERVES 5

PREPARATION TIME: 5 MINUTES, PLUS INFUSING

COOKING TIME: 15 MINUTES

400 ML FULL-FAT MILK

250 ML DOUBLE CREAM

1 CINNAMON STICK

3 STRIPS OF ZEST PARED FROM 1 ORANGE

3 STRIPS OF ZEST PARED FROM 1 LEMON

7 EGG YOLKS

90 G SUGAR

20 G CORNFLOUR

4 TABLESPOONS GRANULATED OR CASTER SUGAR

1 Put the milk, cream, cinnamon stick and orange and lemon zest strips in a pan, making sure there is no white pith on the zest. Bring almost to boiling point before removing from the heat. Cover with cling film and leave to infuse for at least 1 hour.

2 In a separate pan whisk the egg yolks, sugar and cornflour for 3 minutes or until soft and pale in colour. Pour the infused milk through a sieve into the egg mixture, whisking all the time.

3 Place the pan over a medium heat and keep whisking, using a spatula every now and then to clean down the sides of the pan. The mixture should start thickening to a custard consistency. Watch out for the froth – when it's almost at the point when it turns to custard the froth disappears. Reduce the heat right down and keep whisking, otherwise you will end up with sweet scrambled eggs.

4 Pour the custard into ramekins or small terracotta dishes and leave to cool down. Just before serving, sprinkle the tops with some caster sugar and caramelize it with a blowtorch. Alternatively, place the ramekins under a very hot grill until the sugar turns golden and starts to bubble.

ARROZ CON LECHE
RICE PUDDING

SERVES 4

PREPARATION TIME: 5 MINUTES

COOKING TIME: 35 MINUTES

1 LITRE FULL-FAT MILK

1/2 CINNAMON STICK

1 VANILLA POD, SEEDS SCRAPED,
OR 1 TEASPOON VANILLA EXTRACT

1 LEMON, ZEST PARED INTO STRIPS

100 G SPANISH BOMBA RICE
[SEE PAGE 171]

110 G SUGAR

30 G UNSALTED BUTTER

SUGGESTION

In Spain this is served in different ways depending on the region. You can eat it warm or cold, sprinkled with ground cinnamon or even sprinkled with sugar, which is then caramelized with a blowtorch or under a hot grill.

I don't like making comparisons but in the case of rice pudding, I have to say that no other country's rice pudding even comes close to this Spanish classic. Spain is not a major dairy producer but in Asturias in the north (where most of the cows are) they know a thing or two about making great milky desserts. If you can't find Spanish rice, you can just about get away with using short-grain or pudding rice.

1 Pour the milk into a pan and add the cinnamon stick, vanilla pod or vanilla extract and about 3 strips of lemon zest, making sure there is no white pith attached. Place over a medium to high heat and bring to the boil. Stir the milk a few times as it heats up to stop the bottom burning. Be careful with the milk – it is very fickle and as soon as you turn your back it will suddenly boil over and mess up your hob.

2 Just as the milk starts to bubble and rise up, add the rice and give it a good stir. Allow to simmer for 20 minutes, stirring at all times, and then stir in the sugar and cook for a further 10 minutes.

3 Remove from the heat and add the butter; keep stirring so that the butter emulsifies as it melts. Remove and discard the lemon zest strips and the cinnamon stick and vanilla pod (if using) and allow to cool, stirring every 30 minutes or so. Rice pudding is as much about texture as it is about flavour, which is why we add the butter at the end and stir it as it cools.

PERAS AL VINO

PEARS COOKED IN WINE

SERVES 5

PREPARATION TIME: 5 MINUTES

COOKING TIME: 30 MINUTES, PLUS COOLING

5 PEARS, PEELED BUT LEFT WHOLE

1 BOTTLE CHEAP RED OR WHITE WINE [SEE NOTE]

200 G SUGAR

½ CINNAMON STICK

Increasingly these days I find that the supermarkets are filled with exotic fruits that have been flown in from some distant country. To me, these are nothing compared to the wide variety of apples and pears grown all over Spain and throughout the UK. I love this dessert as it is so simple. It also works well with peaches.

1 Slice the bottom off each pear so that they stand up easily. Place them in a small, deep-sided pan so that they fit quite tightly. Add the wine, sugar and cinnamon stick and place over a medium to high heat.

2 Bring to the boil and allow to simmer for 20–30 minutes, or until the pears have softened a bit – they should still be quite firm so take care not to overcook them. Leave to cool down completely in the wine, ideally overnight so that the flavours have time to infuse and penetrate.

3 These pears are delicious on their own but you could also serve them with vanilla ice cream for a more complete dessert. If you want to keep them for longer, place in a sterilized preserving jar, close the lid tightly and boil for 10 minutes. They should then keep for up to six months.

NOTE

You don't need to use expensive wine for this dish and it is equally good with red or white wine. However, if you do fancy something special, try using a Malvasia or Moscatel wine – you should notice the difference in taste.

UVAS AL PEDRO XIMÉNEZ Y CREMA DE TETILLA

GRAPES POACHED IN SWEET SHERRY

SERVES 4

PREPARATION TIME: 5 MINUTES

COOKING TIME: 15 MINUTES, PLUS CHILLING

300 ML PEDRO XIMÉNEZ SWEET SHERRY

50 G SUGAR

200 G RED OR WHITE GRAPES

FOR THE CREAM

400 ML DOUBLE CREAM

100 G TETILLA CHEESE, CHOPPED [SEE NOTE]

70 G SUGAR

Poached grapes in sweet sherry with whipped cheese cream stole my heart recently.

1 Start by making the cream. Put the double cream, cheese and sugar in a small pan over a medium heat and bring to the boil. While still on the heat, use a stick blender to blitz until you have a smooth and creamy texture. Pass through a sieve and chill in the refrigerator for at least 4 hours.

2 Pour the sherry and sugar into a separate pan and place over a medium heat. Bring to the boil and let it boil for 5 minutes before adding the grapes. Return to the boil and simmer for a couple of minutes before removing from the heat. Allow to cool down before chilling in the fridge.

3 To serve, divide the grapes between four small bowls or glass dishes, along with their sherry syrup. Give the cheese cream a final whisk and place a dollop on top of each serving of grapes.

NOTE

If you can't get hold of Tetilla cheese, substitute with Manchego – the result will be just as good.

TARTA ASADA DE QUESO FRESCO Y MORAS

BLACKBERRY CHEESECAKE

SERVES 6

PREPARATION TIME: 5 MINUTES

COOKING TIME: 30 MINUTES

BUTTER, FOR GREASING

300 G CREAM CHEESE

3 EGGS

200 ML DOUBLE CREAM

200 G CASTER SUGAR

100 G BLACKBERRIES

20 G ICING SUGAR (OPTIONAL)

You can make this blackberry cheesecake using pretty much any soft cheese; cream cheese, cottage cheese, quark or curd will all give great results.

1 Preheat the oven to 180°C/gas mark 4 and lightly grease a 20-cm cake tin with a little butter.

2 Put the cream cheese, eggs, cream and sugar into a bowl and use an electric whisk or hand blender to mix together for no longer than 40 seconds.

3 Tip the mixture into your prepared dish and spread the blackberries on top. Bake in the preheated oven for about 30 minutes, or until a knife inserted into the middle comes out clean. Remove from the oven and allow to cool. Dust with icing sugar before serving.

BIENMESABE
ALMOND AND EGG YOLK CREAM

SERVES 5
PREPARATION TIME: 5 MINUTES
COOKING TIME: 20 MINUTES

250 G SUGAR

500 ML WATER

150 G GROUND ALMONDS

PINCH OF GROUND CINNAMON

FINELY GRATED ZEST OF 1/2 LEMON

4 EGG YOLKS

NOTE
This is incredibly tasty and sweet – use it to spread on bread or serve it with flan or ice cream.

I discovered this on a trip to the Canary Islands. I was about 14 at the time and I instantly fell in love with it. I remember trying it in a restaurant and just going straight to the kitchen and asking for the recipe – this has been my modus operandi ever since. Bienmesabe is typical of the way that Arabs prepared their sweets and is a real 'high-energy' treat. Eat in small quantities!

1 First make a syrup. Put the sugar and water in a small, heavy-based pan and place over a high heat; stir to dissolve and let boil for 5 minutes. Add the ground almonds, cinnamon and lemon zest. Cook for a further 10 minutes on a low heat, stirring every so often to stop it sticking to the bottom of the pan.

2 Whisk the egg yolks in a bowl and gradually pour in the almond-syrup mixture, whisking until it is completely combined. Return to a low heat and cook for 3 minutes, stirring all the time with a spoon or spatula – you need to cook the egg yolks just a little but take care not to overcook. The end result should have the texture of a thick marmalade.

FILLOAS CON CREMA
CRÊPES FILLED WITH VANILLA CREAM

SERVES 5

**PREPARATION TIME:
15 MINUTES, PLUS CHILLING**

COOKING TIME: 10 MINUTES

FOR THE CRÊPES

130 G PLAIN FLOUR

PINCH OF SALT

1 EGG

300 ML FULL-FAT MILK
OR CHICKEN STOCK
[SEE ABOVE]

OIL OR BUTTER FOR FRYING

CASTER SUGAR AND GROUND
CINNAMON FOR DUSTING

FOR THE FILLING

500 ML FULL-FAT MILK

1 VANILLA POD, SEEDS
SCRAPED OR 1 TABLESPOON
VANILLA EXTRACT

1 LEMON, ZEST PARED

4 EGG YOLKS

120 G CASTER SUGAR

50 G CORNFLOUR

50 G UNSALTED BUTTER, DICED

These Galician-style crêpes filled with crème patissière are traditionally made using stock from the Caldo Gallego (see page 153).

1 Start by making the filling. Pour the milk into a small pan and add the vanilla pod and seeds (or vanilla extract) and 3 strips of lemon zest. Bring to almost boiling point, remove from the heat and set aside to infuse.

2 Whisk the egg yolks in a bowl with the sugar and cornflour until pale and frothy. Remove the vanilla pod and lemon zest from the milk and slowly pour the infused milk into the egg yolk mixture, whisking all the time. Return to the pan and place over a medium heat. Cook until it has thickened, whisking in the pieces of diced butter one at a time. Take care not to overcook it. This should take about 5 minutes. Allow to cool before chilling in the fridge for 1 hour.

3 To make the crêpes, sift the flour and salt into a bowl, make a well in the centre and add the egg and about half the milk. Stir gently until you have a smooth mixture and then slowly whisk in the remaining milk.

4 Place a non-stick frying pan over a medium heat and drizzle in a little oil or butter; tilt the pan so that the surface is covered. Add a ladleful of crêpe batter, enough to cover the surface of the pan, and cook for 30–45 seconds. Flip the crêpe over and cook the other side. Transfer to a plate and continue making crêpes until all the batter is used up.

5 Fill each crêpe with the crème patissière filling and roll up. Sprinkle with a little caster sugar mixed with ground cinnamon and serve.

CHURROS CON CHOCOLATE

SPANISH DOUGHNUTS WITH CHOCOLATE

SERVES 4

PREPARATION TIME: 30 MINUTES

COOKING TIME: 10 MINUTES

400 ML WATER

400 G STRONG WHITE FLOUR

PINCH OF SALT

1 TABLESPOON OLIVE OIL

750 ML VEGETABLE OIL
FOR DEEP-FRYING

CASTER SUGAR AND GROUND
CINNAMON [OPTIONAL]
FOR DUSTING

FOR THE CHOCOLATE

1 SMALL BAG OF SPANISH
CHOCOLATE POWDER FOR
HOT DIPPING CHOCOLATE

1 PINT MILK

50 G DARK CHOCOLATE,
ROUGHLY CHOPPED

This is not a recipe for the faint-hearted as it involves frying in very hot oil. In Spain you would find a 'churrería' in every town, where these hot, crisp, doughnut sticks are served with rich hot chocolate. Churros is one of those recipes that could go either way but stick to the recipe and follow my advice and you will be fine. I have made thousands of these – trust me!

1 Bring the water to the boil. Meanwhile place the flour and salt in a large pan and place over a very low heat. Stir lightly for 3–4 minutes so that the flour dries out and becomes fluffy.

2 As soon as the water has boiled, pour it over the flour and mix it with a wooden spoon for about 1 minute until a dough starts to form. Don't over-mix and don't worry if there are still some lumps in it as you can always finish it by hand once it has cooled down slightly. Halfway through mixing add the olive oil.

3 When the dough is still warm, knead for 1 minute. Place in a piping bag (not plastic) with a 8-point star-shaped nozzle and spread out a sheet of baking parchment. Start squeezing the batter on to the parchment to make the churros. Let me warn you: it's hard work so make sure you don't strain any muscles. At this point you could freeze the churros and cook later (they can be cooked straight from the freezer).

Continued overleaf.

4 Heat the vegetable oil in a large deep pan – ideally you want it to be 230–240°C to get that delicious crispy outside and soft interior. To test whether the oil is hot enough, drop a small piece of the dough into the oil – if it immediately floats to the surface and starts fizzing away then the oil is hot enough. If it sinks, wait a little longer.

5 Once the oil is hot enough carefully slide your churros, a few at a time, into the pan. Cook them for 40 seconds on one side and 30 seconds on the other. Remove and drain on kitchen paper and repeat until all your churros are cooked. They should be very crispy on the outside and moist on the inside. Make sure the temperature of the oil doesn't drop, as your churros will not cook properly. Dust liberally with sugar mixed with a little ground cinnamon (optional) while they are still warm.

6 For the chocolate, just bring the milk to the boil in a pot and just before boiling point add the chocolate powder while whisking. Stir constantly for 10 minutes so the chocolate doesn't burn on the bottom of the pot. Stir in the dark chocolate at the end to give nice body and intensify the flavour. Serve the chocolate in a cup and dip your churros in it.

TRUFAS DE CHOCOLATE Y ACEITUNAS

CHOCOLATE AND OLIVE TRUFFLES

MAKES 25

PREPARATION TIME: 10 MINUTES, PLUS CHILLING

COOKING TIME: 5 MINUTES

100 G DOUBLE CREAM

100 G DARK (70%) CHOCOLATE, BROKEN INTO PIECES

ZEST OF ½ ORANGE

30 G PITTED BLACK OLIVES, FINELY CHOPPED

20 G BUTTER, DICED

COCOA POWDER FOR DUSTING

NOTE

I love the intensity of the black olives and the contrast of the savoury and sweet here, but you can flavour these truffles with almost anything.

These chocolate and Spanish olive truffles were a bit of a revelation to me. I'd never seen it done before and just decided to go for it. The result is surprisingly delicious.

1 Place the cream in a pan over a medium heat and bring to almost boiling point. Remove from the heat and add the chocolate, orange zest and black olives and mix well with a spatula until you get a smooth texture. At this point the mix should still be warm. Add the diced butter and stir well to combine to give shine and silkiness to the truffle mixture.

2 Cover with cling film and refrigerate for a few hours (the mixture will be easier to handle when it has chilled). Roll small balls of the mixture between your hands. Dust liberally with cocoa powder and return to the fridge – enjoy them cold as they will take longer to melt in your mouth!

TARTA DE SANTIAGO

ALMOND TART

SERVES 8

PREPARATION TIME: 10 MINUTES

COOKING TIME: 35 MINUTES

4 EGGS

250 G SUGAR

250 G COARSELY GROUND ALMONDS

PINCH OF GROUND CINNAMON

1 SHOT OF RUM [OPTIONAL]

50 G BUTTER, SOFTENED

1 TABLESPOON ICING SUGAR

1 Preheat the oven to 170°C/gas mark 4.

2 Whisk the eggs with the sugar until pale and frothy. Add the ground almonds, cinnamon, rum and softened butter and whisk until you have a soft creamy mixture.

3 Grease a round cake tin, about 30 cm in diameter, with a little butter and pour in the cake mix. Bake in the preheated oven for about 35 minutes, or until firm to the touch. Allow to cool in the tin for a few minutes before turning on to a wire rack and dusting with icing sugar.

POLVORONES
CHRISTMAS BISCUITS

MAKES 8

PREPARATION TIME: 15 MINUTES

COOKING TIME: 30 MINUTES

75 G GROUND ALMONDS

140 G PLAIN FLOUR

90 G LARD OR BUTTER

50 G ICING SUGAR

1 TEASPOON GROUND CINNAMON

Even though these are traditional Christmas biscuits, that has never stopped me from making them all year round. They are not too sweet and, of course, I love anything with almonds...

1 Preheat the oven to 170°C/gas mark 3. Spread the ground almonds and flour in a baking tray and toast in the oven for about 15 minutes or until light brown, stirring the flour and almonds every few minutes so that everything toasts evenly. Leave to cool down to room temperature.

2 Mix together the lard or butter, icing sugar, ground cinnamon and toasted flour until it comes together in a dough, this should take about 5 minutes. You can use a food processor for this or do it by hand.

3 Use a rolling pin to roll out the dough on a floured surface to a thickness of 2 cm. Cut out round biscuit shapes, squeezing them a bit between your hands.

4 Transfer to a baking tray and bake in the preheated oven for about 14 minutes, until they are crisp and golden. Allow to cool. Traditionally these biscuits would be wrapped in little parcels of thin greaseproof paper and given as gifts.

THE CHEF'S CUT ★9

TORTILLITAS DE CAMARONES

MINI SHRIMP PANCAKES

SERVES 4 AS A TAPA

PREPARATION TIME: 10 MINUTES

COOKING TIME: 5 MINUTES

75 G PLAIN FLOUR

75 G CHICKPEA FLOUR

1 TEASPOON SALT

PINCH OF BLACK PEPPER

200 ML COLD WATER

3 SPRING ONIONS, FINELY CHOPPED

2 TABLESPOONS FRESHLY CHOPPED FLAT-LEAF PARSLEY

100 G PEELED 1 CM-LONG SHRIMPS [SEE NOTE]

VEGETABLE OIL FOR FRYING

These traditional crispy prawn 'pancakes' from Cadiz are so addictive. They are the perfect snack to eat with friends and a few beers on a sunny day.

1 Place the flours, salt and black pepper in a large bowl and whisk in the water, a little at a time, until you have a smooth pancake batter. Add the chopped spring onions, parsley and shrimps and mix again.

2 Pour vegetable oil into a large wide frying pan to a depth of about 2 cm and place over a high heat. The oil needs to reach a temperature of 190°C – to test if it is hot enough pour a drop of batter into the oil; it should sizzle vigorously and rise to the surface. Use a tablespoon to pour spoonfuls of the batter into the pan – each spoonful will be one 'tortillita'. Cook in batches of 3 or 4 at a time, depending on the size of your pan. Fry for 1 minute on each side until golden and crisp.

3 Drain on kitchen paper and enjoy with a refreshing cold cerveza.

NOTE

If you can't find these minuscule shrimps, use small peeled prawns and chop them finely.

PULPO A LA GALLEGA

OCTOPUS WITH POTATOES AND PIMENTÓN

SERVES 4 AS A TAPA
PREPARATION TIME: 5 MINUTES
COOKING TIME: 30 MINUTES

1 KG SMALL OCTOPUS, DEFROSTED

200 G NEW POTATOES, IDEALLY ALL THE SAME SIZE

SEA SALT FLAKES

1 TEASPOON SWEET PIMENTÓN

DRIZZLE OF EXTRA-VIRGIN OLIVE OIL (SPANISH, IF POSSIBLE)

COOKING OCTOPUS

The bigger the octopus the longer it takes to cook:

1 kg – 25 minutes
2 kg – 35 minutes
3 kg – 40 minutes
4 kg and above – 45 minutes

In my opinion octopus is one of Spain's greatest delicacies – again, that is one of the reasons why we do so little to it. Simplicity at its best.

1 Clean the octopus by shaking it under cold running water so that you wash away any sand trapped in its tentacles. Remove the brain and beak. Bring a large pan of water to the boil.

2 Grab the octopus by the head with a pair of tongs and plunge as much of the octopus as you can into the boiling water and quickly bring it back up above the water for 5 seconds. Repeat this move three times before finally dropping into the boiling water. The idea is to warm the octopus slowly without the skin breaking.

3 Boil the octopus for about 20–30 minutes until tender, although the cooking time will vary depending on the size of the octopus. You can spot when an octopus is ready by looking at and feeling the tentacles – they should be soft and floppy with no resistance. Approximately halfway through the cooking time add the new potatoes – the potatoes should cook in about 15 minutes so you might need to calculate your cooking time depending on the size of your octopus (see left).

4 Drain the new potatoes and octopus and slice them both into 1-cm slices. Scatter with sea salt flakes and the pimentón and drizzle generously with good olive oil.

CARACOLES ESTOFADOS

SNAILS WITH SERRANO HAM, CHORIZO AND CHILLIES

SERVES 5 AS A TAPA
PREPARATION TIME: 30 MINUTES
COOKING TIME: 1–2 HOURS

1 KG SNAILS

100 G JAMÓN SERRANO, DICED

1 SEMI-DRIED CHORIZO SAUSAGE, CHOPPED

1 GUINDILLA CHILLI OR 2 DRIED CAYENNE PEPPERS

4 SPRIGS OF FRESH THYME

SPRIG OF FRESH OREGANO

8 CORIANDER SEEDS

PINCH OF FRESHLY GRATED NUTMEG

4 BLACK PEPPERCORNS

1 TEASPOON SALT

100 ML OLIVE OIL

1 SLICE OF BREAD

4 GARLIC CLOVES, PEELED BUT LEFT WHOLE

1 ONION, FINELY CHOPPED

2 TOMATOES, CHOPPED

1 TEASPOON SWEET PIMENTÓN

1 PIMIENTO CHORICERO, SOAKED IN HOT WATER [OPTIONAL, SEE PAGE 52]

200 ML DRY WHITE WINE

There are some dishes that seem to sum up a holiday experience, particularly if it's somewhere you travel to again and again. For me, the place is Agua Amarga, a tiny village in Almería in Andalucía, and the dish is stewed snails in Bar Felipe, a very crowded bar with the nicest camareros (bar staff). When I have it, I truly feel on holiday.

1 Thoroughly scrub the snails under cold running water and place them in a large pot. Cover with cold water and place over a low heat. After about 15–20 minutes the snails will start to come out of their shells as they feel comfortable in the warm water. At this point increase the heat to high and let them boil for 1 minute. Drain, return to the pan, just cover with fresh cold water and simmer again over a low heat.

2 Add the jamón serrano, chorizo, guindilla or cayenne peppers, thyme, oregano, coriander seeds, nutmeg, peppercorns and salt. Cover with a lid and leave to simmer.

3 Meanwhile, heat about half the olive oil in a small pan and fry the bread on both sides until crisp and golden. Remove from the pan and set aside. Add the remaining oil and fry the garlic cloves until light golden, then add the chopped onion. After a few minutes add the chopped tomatoes and pimentón. If you are using the pimiento choricero, scrape the pulp from the inside and add to the pan. Cook for 10 minutes over a low heat, then add the fried bread and white wine. Simmer for 5 minutes and then transfer to a blender and blitz until you have a smooth purée.

4 Add this purée to the pot of snails and let it all simmer together for around 1–2 hours, depending on the size. Check for doneness every 10 minutes or so – they should be tender but still have some bounce, sitting in a thick sauce.

5 Tip into a large shallow dish and serve with plenty of bread and snail forks (a needle will also do) to pick the snails out of their shells.

LENGUAS DE CORDERO GUISADAS
BRAISED LAMBS' TONGUES

SERVES 4

PREPARATION TIME: 20 MINUTES

COOKING TIME: 2½ HOURS

12–16 LAMBS' TONGUES, DEPENDING ON SIZE

50 ML OLIVE OIL OR LARD

5 GARLIC CLOVES, PEELED BUT LEFT WHOLE

1 ONION, ROUGHLY CHOPPED

4 CARROTS, PEELED AND CHOPPED

4 BLACK PEPPERCORNS

1 BAY LEAF

1 CLOVE

4 SPRIGS OF THYME

2 TOMATOES, CHOPPED

200 ML WHITE WINE

2 POTATOES, PEELED AND ROUGHLY CHOPPED

1 TEASPOON SALT

In Spain we love to use all parts of the animal, but they need to be treated with care to get the best out of them. These lambs' tongues are delicious and soft when stewed for a long time. This recipe is about as traditional as it gets. You can also make it with pigs' tongues.

1 Start by washing the tongues under cold running water for a couple of minutes. Place them in a pan with 1 litre of cold water and boil them for 15 minutes. Drain, reserving the water. While the tongues are still hot, peel away the rough outer skin using a small knife.

2 Heat the olive oil or lard in the same pan over a medium heat and add the tongues. Brown on all sides – this should take about 6 minutes – and remove from the pan. Add the garlic, onion, carrot, peppercorns, bay leaf, clove and thyme and cook for a few minutes until light golden in colour.

3 Add the chopped tomatoes and reduce for 2 minutes. Return the tongues to the pan and add the white wine and the water reserved from cooking the tongues. Season, cover and simmer over a low heat for 1 hour.

4 After 1 hour add the potatoes to the pan – everything should fit quite tightly. Put the lid back on and simmer for a further 1 hour. Taste and adjust the seasoning and check if the tongues and potatoes are cooked – they should be soft.

CANGREJOS DE RÍO EN SALSA
CRAYFISH MY AUNTY'S WAY

SERVES 4

PREPARATION TIME: 10 MINUTES

COOKING TIME: 10 MINUTES

1 KG LIVE FRESH CRAYFISH

100 ML OLIVE OIL

1 ONION, FINELY CHOPPED

1 BAY LEAF

5 GARLIC CLOVES, FINELY CHOPPED

1 GUINDILLA DRIED CHILLI [ANY DRIED CHILLI WILL DO], CHOPPED

1 TEASPOON SWEET PIMENTÓN

1 TEASPOON SALT

FRESHLY CRACKED WHITE PEPPER

1 TEASPOON FLOUR

50 ML BRANDY

FRESH BREAD, TO SERVE

FOR THE MAJADA SAUCE

1 TABLESPOON BLANCHED ALMONDS

2 SPRIGS OF PARSLEY

200 ML WHITE WINE

As a kid I used to go with my parents to the Pardo woods (on the outskirts of Madrid) to pick red pine mushrooms and to find crayfish. This family tradition gave rise to this delicious recipe.

1 Start by rinsing the crayfish in cold running water and leave to drain in a colander.

2 Make the majada by pounding together all the ingredients, using either a pestle and mortar or a food processor, until you have a smooth purée. Gather together all your ingredients and utensils as this recipe is very quick to prepare and you will need everything to hand.

3 Heat the oil in a large, wide pan over a medium heat and add the onions and bay leaf. Sweat until golden, about 5 minutes and then add the garlic. Cook for a further 3 minutes, add the chopped dried chilli, pimentón, salt, a few twists of white pepper and the flour and cook, stirring, for 1 minute.

4 Add the whole crayfish to the pan, pour the brandy over and flambé quickly by setting light to the pan with a lighter or some long matches; shake the pan for 10 seconds. Now add the majada sauce and flambé again, shaking the pan until the flames have died down. Pour in about 200 ml water and cover the pan with a lid; continue to shake the pan over the heat for about 3 minutes so that the crayfish move around in the pan and so cook evenly (crayfish shouldn't take longer than 5 minutes to cook from start to finish). Enjoy with lots of bread.

CALLOS A LA MADRILEÑA

STEWED BEEF TRIPE

SERVES 8

PREPARATION TIME: 30 MINUTES

COOKING TIME: 3¼ HOURS

2 KG BEEF TRIPE (TRY ETHNIC BUTCHERS)

1 KG COWS' TROTTERS (AS ABOVE), HALVED

200 G PANCETA CURADA (CURED PORK BELLY)

200 G JAMÓN SERRANO (CURED HAM), IN A PIECE, NOT SLICED

3 PIGS' TROTTERS

4 BLACK PEPPERCORNS

1 CLOVE

Ladies and gentlemen, let me introduce you to a dish to die for – Madrid-style beef tripe stew. I'm not joking: I've seen people fighting for the last plate of this incredible stew. Be aware – you need to have a taste for gelatinous types of food, as this dish is all about that. As you will have gathered by now, in Spain we love turning the ugly parts of the animal into something beautiful. The hardest part will be shopping for the ingredients; the preparation itself is very simple.

1 Most of the tripe you find today will have been cleaned, blanched and vacuum packed. If you do buy it fresh, discard any ugly bits attached to the tripe bag, scrub them with coarse sea salt between your hands and then boil in a large pan with a glass of cheap white vinegar for 10 minutes. Drain and then chop into 2-cm squares.

2 Place the tripe pieces in a large, wide pan with the cows' trotter halves, panceta curada, jamón serrano, pigs' trotters, peppercorns, clove and bay leaves and cover with cold water. Bring to the boil and simmer gently (it will take about 3 hours for all the meats to be cooked and soft).

3 Meanwhile, heat the olive oil in a separate pan and gently fry the garlic cloves for 1 minute. Add the dried chillies and sauté for a further minute. Add the onion and cook for about 10 minutes, or until translucent but not browned. Add the ground cumin, pimentón and thyme leaves and stir through before adding the chopped tomato. Reduce down for about 5 minutes.

4 After the tripe has been simmering for 1 hour add the morcilla, chorizo and the onion, garlic and tomato mixture. Let it all simmer together for about 2 more hours. Remove the panceta, morcilla, chorizo, trotter and snout from the pan and chop into rough chunks, taking care not to burn your fingers. Return the chopped pieces to the pan and bring back to the boil. Cook for 15 minutes and then serve.

NOTE

This dish tastes even better the day after you have cooked it, as the flavours keep developing within the stew. I always make this in large quantities so I can still eat it 4 days later (because of the fat and gelatine it will keep for a few days).

2 BAY LEAVES

50 ML OLIVE OIL

3 GARLIC CLOVES, PEELED BUT LEFT WHOLE

2 HOT DRIED CHILLIES, CRUMBLED

1 ONION, FINELY CHOPPED

1 TEASPOON GROUND CUMIN

1 TABLESPOON SWEET PIMENTÓN

5 SPRIGS OF THYME, LEAVES PICKED

1 TOMATO, FINELY CHOPPED

1 MORCILLA DE CEBOLLA [BLACK PUDDING MADE WITH ONION, NOT RICE]

1 FRESH CHORIZO SAUSAGE

ENSALADA DE MORCILLA Y QUESO

BLACK PUDDING AND GOATS' CHEESE SALAD

SERVES 4

PREPARATION TIME: 5 MINUTES

COOKING TIME: 5–6 MINUTES

200 G WATERCRESS
OR LAMB'S LETTUCE

1 SMALL PUNNET RASPBERRIES,
ABOUT 200 G

2 TABLESPOONS PINE NUTS,
TOASTED

1 TABLESPOON OLIVE OIL

200 G SOFT GOATS' CHEESE,
SLICED INTO 1-CM ROUNDS

1 MORCILLA DE BURGOS
(BLOOD SAUSAGE), SLICED
INTO 1-CM ROUNDS

FOR THE DRESSING

1 TEASPOON CLEAR HONEY

3 TABLESPOONS OLIVE OIL

1 TABLESPOON SHERRY VINEGAR

SALT AND FRESHLY GROUND
BLACK PEPPER

1 Wash and dry the watercress and toss with the berries and pine nuts.

2 Heat 1 tablespoon of oil in a non-stick pan over a medium to high heat. Pan-fry the goats' cheese slices on one side only, until golden. Remove from the pan and then pan-fry the morcilla for about 2 minutes on each side. Remove from the pan and drain on kitchen paper. Add the goats' cheese and morcilla slices to the salad.

3 Whisk together the ingredients for the dressing or put them into an empty jar with a lid and shake vigorously. Pour over the salad and serve immediately.

COCHINILLO ASADO CON PATATAS PANADERA

ROAST SUCKLING PIG WITH POTATOES

SERVES 6–8

PREPARATION TIME: 15 MINUTES

COOKING TIME: 2 HOURS

1 SUCKLING PIG, ABOUT 4–5 KG

2 TABLESPOONS ROCK SALT

8 LARGE POTATOES,
PEELED AND SLICED THICKLY

1 SPANISH ONION, THINLY SLICED

6 GARLIC CLOVES, UNPEELED
AND CRUSHED LIGHTLY

4 BAY LEAVES

2 SPRIGS OF THYME,
LEAVES PICKED

OLIVE OIL

SALT AND FRESHLY GROUND
BLACK PEPPER

Cooking milk-fed pig or lamb is not just a meal, it's an event. This is the kind of thing we do just once or twice a year. It is a real delicacy but so easy to make at the same time. These young animals can be hard to get outside Spain but it is worth trying – any good butcher should be able to get hold of them for you.

1 Preheat the oven to 170°/gas mark 3.

2 Use a blowtorch to burn any hair from the skin of the pig and cut down the middle, from nose to tail, with a sharp knife, so that the head and tail are still intact (you may want to ask your butcher to do this). Open the pig out like a book and rub rock salt all over the skin on both halves of the pig. Place it, skin-side down, on an oiled oven rack. You don't want the skin to stick and break when turning over.

3 Mix the sliced potatoes and onion with the garlic, bay leaves, fresh thyme and salt and pepper and tip into a large roasting tin or terracotta dish. Pour over enough olive oil to come halfway up the potatoes and then slide the dish into the oven, positioned underneath the rack with the suckling pig on. The idea is that as the suckling pig cooks, all the juices will drip down into the potatoes.

4 After 1 hour turn the pig halves over and pierce the skin with a fork; use a large spoon to turn the potatoes. Continue to roast for another hour, turning the potatoes once again, until the meat is tender, the skin golden and the potatoes cooked.

5 Drain the potatoes from the oil and serve with a good piece of suckling pig. By the end of the cooking time the meat should be so moist and tender that no sauce is needed.

NOTE

In Spain we would usually cook this dish in a wood-fired oven, so it acquires that smoky aroma characteristic of cooking with wood.

MANITAS DE CERDO ESTOFADAS CON MEMBRILLO

PIG TROTTERS WITH QUINCE

SERVES 3

PREPARATION TIME: 20 MINUTES

COOKING TIME: 2¼ HOURS

100 ML OLIVE OIL

3 PIG TROTTERS, SLICED IN HALF [ASK YOUR BUTCHER TO DO THIS FOR YOU]

1 QUINCE, WASHED, QUARTERED AND CORED

1 ONION, ROUGHLY CHOPPED

1 CARROT, PEELED AND ROUGHLY CHOPPED

1 LEEK, ROUGHLY CHOPPED

4 GARLIC CLOVES, PEELED AND LEFT WHOLE

1 TOMATO, CHOPPED

1 TABLESPOON BROWN SUGAR

1 BAY LEAF

4 SPRIGS OF THYME, LEAVES PICKED

200 ML RED WINE

1 LITRE BEEF STOCK

SALT AND FRESHLY GROUND BLACK PEPPER

BREAD, TO SERVE

Prepare to enjoy soft braised pig trotters with a sticky, sweet sauce and whole pieces of soft quince.

1 Heat the olive oil in a wide frying pan over a high heat and fry the trotters on all sides until browned. Remove from the pan and set aside.

2 Add the quartered quince to the pan and fry on all three sides until browned. Set aside. Add the onion, carrot, leek and garlic cloves and fry until browned, about 5 minutes. Then add the chopped tomato, brown sugar, bay leaf and thyme and give it a stir.

3 Add the red wine and boil for about 2 minutes, until reduced by half, and then add the beef stock. Add the trotters, salt and pepper and bring to the boil. Simmer over a medium heat for about 2 hours, adding the pan-fried quince pieces to the pan after 1 hour (you don't want the quince to turn to mush). Serve with plenty of bread to dip into the sauce.

INDEX

A

alioli 44–5
  mayonnaise-style 45
  my favourite 46
  traditional 46
almond 10
  caramelized 10
  chilled soup 148
  & egg yolk cream 198
  salted 10
  tart 204
anchovy
  & caramelized onion tart 138
  marinated 14
apple & red cabbage 142
artichoke
  & asparagus 'Granada'
    style 122
  & lamb shanks 104–5
asparagus
  & artichokes 'Granada'
    style 122
  with Serrano ham 124
aubergine, tomato, pepper
  & cod 50–1

B

bacon 95, 98, 108, 179
bean stew, Asturian 180
beef 96–7, 158–9
  braised, & potatoes 113
  tripe, stewed 214–15
beer-braised ribs 108
biscuits, Christmas 205
black pudding 158–9
  bacon, chorizo & fried
    bread 98
  & goat's cheese salad
    216–17
blackberry cheesecake 196
bread
  fried, with bacon, chorizo
    & black pudding 98

mum's eggy 184
  scrubbed with garlic &
    tomato 18

C

cabbage
  braised red, & apple 142
  & potato cakes 132
caramel 188–9
cheese & tomato paste 26
cheesecake, blackberry 196
chicken 158–9, 165–7, 172
  garlicky 78
  grapes, red wine &
    chestnuts 84
  Moorish 81
  & red pepper stew 80
  with Spanish olives 83
  wings, sweet wine &
    prunes 76–7
chilli sauce, garlic & cod
  54–6
chocolate
  morcilla sausage &
    crashed eggs 68
  & olive truffles 203
  & Spanish doughnuts
    200–2
  with venison 114
chorizo 6, 7, 73, 108, 153,
  158–9, 172, 179–80
  black pudding, bacon
    & fried bread 98
  chillies, Serrano ham
    & snails 210–11
  with cider 88
  potato & peppers 156
  prawn & crashed eggs 68
Christmas biscuits 205
cider
  with chorizo 88
  cod in 57
cinnamon sugar 184

clam(s)
  garlic & parsley 37
  sherry & ham 38
cod
  in cider 57
  garlic & chilli sauce
    54–6
  peas & parsley 59
  peppers, aubergines
    & tomatoes 50–1
  & piquillo peppers 53
  in rich pepper sauce 52
  in white sauce, peppers
    stuffed with 131
cows' trotters 214–15
crayfish my aunty's way 213
cream
  almond & egg yolk 198
  vanilla, & crêpes 199
crème caramel, 'the' 188
crêpes & vanilla cream 199
croquettes, ham 90–4
custard
  -filled puffs 186–7
  Catalan pots 190

D

dips, chilled tomato 20
doughnuts, Spanish,
  & chocolate 200–2

E

egg(s) 70–3, 189
  baked, & pan-fried peppers
    75
  crashed 66–8
  fried 69
  fried, & ratatouille 125
  mum's eggy bread 184
  peas & Serrano ham 120
  scrambled, & young
    garlic 74
  yolk, & almond cream 198

F

fat from heaven 189
fennel & orange salad 139
fish
    Catalonian stew 152
    fried 34–6
    see also specific fish

G

gammon 153, 180
garlic
    chilli sauce & cod 54–6
    garlicky chicken 78
    mayonnaise 44–6
    mayonnaise potatoes 126
    with mushrooms 136
    parsley, & clams 37
    with prawns 40
    rosemary, Manchego
        & green olives 12
    soup 150
    & tomato scrubbed
        bread 18
    vinegar & sea bass 62–3
    young, & scrambled eggs 74
goat's cheese & black
    pudding salad 216–17
grapes
    poached in sweet sherry 195
    red wine, chestnuts
        & chicken 84

H

ham see Serrano ham
herring & vegetable tart 133
hotpot, Galician 153

J

jelly, quince 22–3

L

lamb
    Arab-style braised leg 103
    braised tongue 212
    roast 106–7
    shank, & artichoke 104–5
langoustine 168–9

lemonade with a twist 27
lentil stew 179
lobster, soupy rice 168–9

M

mackerel, pickled 49
Majada sauce 213
mayonnaise, garlic 44–6
    & potatoes 126
mayonnaise-style alioli 45
meatballs 96–7
mojo picón 111
    & wrinkled potatoes 129–30
mojo verde 129–30
morcilla sausage 180
    bacon, chorizo & fried
        bread 98
    chocolate & crashed eggs 68
mushrooms with garlic 136

N

nut & pepper dip with
    roasted vegetables 118–19

O

octopus, potato & Pimentón
    209
olive
    black, red onion, paprika
        & cumin seeds 14
    & chocolate truffles 203
    green, lemon, oregano
        & chillies 12
    green, Manchego, rosemary
        & garlic 12
    marinated 12–14
    Spanish, with chicken 83
omelette, Spanish 70–3
onion, caramelized, &
    anchovy tart 138
orange & fennel salad 139
oxtail with red wine 115

P

Padrón pepper
    fried 16
    ham & crashed eggs 68

paella
    with pasta 175–6
    'the' 165–7
pancakes, mini shrimp 208
panceta 108, 180
pancetta curada 98, 132,
    179, 214–15
pasta with paella 175–6
pastry, tuna & pepper 140–1
pear, cooked in wine 194
pea(s)
    parsley & cod 59
    Serrano ham & eggs 120
pepper
    aubergine, tomato & cod
        50–1
    chorizo & potato 156
    & nut dip 118–19
    pan-fried, baked with
        eggs 75
    piquillo, & cod 53
    red, & chicken stew 80
    rich sauce, & cod 52
    roasted red 134–5
    sauce (mojo picón) 111,
        129–30
    stuffed with cod in white
        sauce 131
    & tomato chilled soup 146
    & tuna filled pastry 140–1
    see also Padrón pepper
pig, roast suckling, &
    potatoes 218–19
pig trotters 214–15
    with quince 220
Pimentón & peppers with
    octopus 209
pork 96–7
    beer-braised ribs 108
    braised cheeks 101–2
    fillet, skewers 111–12
    see also pig
pork leaf lard 153
potato 66–8, 70–3
    with braised beef 113
    & cabbage cakes 132
    garlic mayonnaise 126

peppers & chorizo 156
Pimentón & octopus 209
poor man's 126
& roast suckling pig
    218–19
wrinkled, & mojos 129–30
prawn 168–71, 175–6
    chorizo & crashed eggs 68
    with garlic 40
    griddled 42
prune, sweet wine & chicken
    wings 76–7
puffs, custard-filled 186–7

Q
quince
    jelly 22–3
    with pig trotters 220

R
rabbit 165–7
    hunter's 95
    sausage & rice 178
ratatouille & fried eggs 125
red cabbage, braised,
    & apple 142
red wine
    chestnuts, grapes &
        chicken 84
    with oxtail 115
ribs, beer-braised 108
rice
    baked with a crust 172
    mellow vegetable 177
    paella with pasta 175–6
    pudding 192
    sausage & rabbit 178
    soupy lobster 168–9
    squid ink 170–1
    'the' paella 165–7

S
salads
    black pudding & goat's
        cheese 216
    fennel & orange 139
sangria, special 30

sausage 172
    white, rabbit & rice 178
    see also morcilla sausage
sea bass with garlic
    & vinegar 62–3
sea bream baked in salt 60
Serrano ham 154–5, 214–15
    with asparagus 124
    chorizo, chillies & snails
        210–11
    croquettes 90–4
    eggs & peas 120
    Padrón pepper & crashed
        eggs 68
    sherry & clams 38
    trout wrapped in 47
sherry
    Serrano ham & clams 38
    sweet, grapes poached
        in 195
shrimp, mini pancakes 208
skewers, Moorish 111–12
snail, Serrano ham, chorizo
    & chillies 210–11
soup
    chilled almond 148
    chilled tomato & pepper
        146
    garlic 150
soupy lobster rice 168–9
squid 168–9, 175–6
squid ink rice 170–1
stew
    Asturian bean 180
    Catalonian fish 152
    chicken & red pepper 80
    lentil 179
    Madrid-style 158–9
    tuna & saffron 151
    vegetable 154–5

T
tarts
    almond 204
    caramelized onion
        & anchovy 138
    herring & vegetable 133

tomato
    & cheese paste 26
    chilled dip 20
    and garlic scrubbed
        bread 18
    pepper, aubergine
        & cod 50–1
    & pepper chilled soup 146
tortilla, potato 70–3
tripe, stewed beef 214–15
trout in Serrano ham 47
truffles, choc & olive 203
tuna
    & pepper filled pastry 140–1
    & saffron stew 151

V
vanilla cream & crêpes 199
vegetable(s)
    & herring tart 133
    mellow rice 177
    roasted, & pepper & nut
        dip 118–19
    stew 154–5
venison with chocolate 114

W
white sauce 131
wine
    pears cooked in 194
    sweet, prunes & chicken
        wings 76–7
    see also red wine

ACKNOWLEDGEMENTS

What a terrific journey this has been, not just for the book but since we started this modest revolution. I would like to thank everyone who has helped me along the way on this crazy mission to spread the word about the food I love the most. It has being tough but I have thoroughly enjoyed every minute of it. With friends like you I can only beg for more …

Ken Sanker: a huge thank you for believing in me from the start and helping me with every step, I wouldn't have made it this far without you. I am immensely grateful.

Douglas and Mac: you guys are awesome, I feel privileged working with you every day. With a team like us, I'm happy to face whatever comes our way.

El equipo: gracias a todos por poner toda la carne en el asador y querer compartir con todo el que pasa por nuestras barras nuestra particular forma de hacer las cosas. Gustavo y Eric, sois el alma de esta historia, gracias por el continuo esfuerzo y entendimiento, espero que sigamos juntos mucho tiempo.

Sarah Lavelle: I know my easy, laid-back approach to life disappears when it comes to work – SURPRISE! But I hope it has all been worth it! Thanks for joining the Tapas Revolution and publishing this book. Thanks for your understanding, for bouncing back ideas and your guidance. It has been great!

The Ebury Team: maybe one too many meetings I know, my fault,

it's my socializing nature you see … Seriously, thank you so much for the team effort, I have felt very supported, I really appreciate it.

Clare Sayer: Thank you for translating my Spanglish into English. I love the way you made it all sound very much like I normally speak and communicate. It wasn't an easy one and you literally nailed it.

Emma, Alex and team: thank you for convincing me to keep it simple, keep the essence – I now understand why. You have created a truly great look for this book. Very well done, guys.

Mr Poole: mate, nothing to do with me, I am not saying this because it's my book, you know how critical I am of myself. I honestly think (and I have done my research) that you have captured the magic of Spanish food better than anyone else in the history of photography. Standing ovation for you! (APPLAUSE). Thank you.

Nicole and Rachel: thank you for the fine and precise job. These outstanding photos wouldn't have been possible without your skill. What a great pleasure it has been working together.

And of course a huge thank you to everyone who, through all the years, has helped me shape my cooking skills, as well as who I am today in one way or another. There is a bit of all you within me, I feel very lucky and I am very proud of it.